MW01295557

Your Foal: Essential Training

"Your Foal: Essential Training"
By Keith Hosman
ISBN: 1478238518
ISBN-13: 978-1478238515

Keith Hosman
horsemanship101.com
PO Box 31
Utopia, TX 78884 USA

100716

Your Foal: Essential Training

By Keith Hosman, John Lyons Certified Trainer

Part of the "Horse Training How-To" Series from Horsemanship101.com
Find step-by-step horse training articles 24/7 at Horsemanship101.com/Articles

Table of Contents

If you were the first person to someday ride your weanling, would you feel safer if the colt did – or did not – have a proper foundation?

Section I: Days 1 – 5
You have years till you can ride your colt or filly – and a lot of training needs to be done in the meantime.

Your foal-training guide

We begin with simple body control.

Sacking Out and Desensitizing

Halter-training Your Foal

Your foal's ground manners today correspond directly to his quality as a riding horse tomorrow. (If he drags on the lead now, he'll ignore your reins entirely later.)

Teach your foal to stand properly for a bath – but also see this as an opportunity to strengthen your position as leader in your herd of two.

Section II: Additional Training
Further training for this stage of your horse's life

Preface

If you were the first person to someday ride your weanling, would you feel safer if the colt did – or did not – have a proper foundation?

Do you have a foal on the way? Maybe you've got a weanling who's growing like a weed – but in need of training and possibly getting dangerous? Do you know what training is essential for baby horses, how to approach the work – and how much is too much?

You have years till you can ride your colt or filly – but there's a lot of training that needs to be done in the meantime. They need to cooperate for the farrier, to stand near you politely, to be led around the barn, to respect your space – they need to become a cheerful member of your family. This book is your step-by-step guide and it shows you exactly what to do, what to look for, and in what order.

Based on the gentle and proven techniques of John Lyons, "Days" 1-5 teach your horse to respect your space, to deal with fear, to stand calmly and to begin "giving to pressure." Take each "day" at a pace you set. Section II contains additional training you might very well need at this stage in your young horse's life.

Putting a strong, solid and well-considered foundation into your foal will pay big dividends later when it comes time to start it to saddle. Remember: You ride the horse you lead – and that training begins today.

And, a couple years from now, when it's time to introduce your horse to a saddle and rider, you'll begin the next phase of your horse's training in the round pen. My book "Round Penning: First Steps to Starting a Horse" can then be your guide; it's a step-by-step roadmap to the training you'll need to do. By way of introduction, I've included an entire chapter from that book at the end of this book, a chapter that'll " Teach Your Horse to Come to You."

Good luck in your training!

Keith Hosman
John Lyons Certified Trainer
Utopia, Texas USA

Section I: Days 1 – 5

You have years till you can ride your colt or filly – and a lot of training needs to be done in the meantime.

Introduction

Your foal-training guide

Weanlings are like hot house flowers. There's only so much you can do with them while you're waiting for them to grow and blossom into something you can ride or ask to pull a cart. You feed them; you water them; you show them off. Still, potted plants don't grow progressively more dangerous with each passing day as can the typical colt beginning to feel his oats. Few florists are done in annually by your average petunia, yet growing your horse into a safe and obliging member of the family requires buckets of consistent training from you, the owner. Loving horse owners are done in frequently by well-placed kicks; they lose fingers to "playful nips" and have their toes stepped on all too often. For safety's sake – and to ensure his value in future years as a quality "riding horse," there are certain training milestones that must be met as we wait for them to grow into "something we can use."

If you could simply throw the horse into a pasture and come back two or three years later with a saddle, you could forgo this book – but that's not really possible. Above the simple fact that we'd like to pet our baby and hang out with him, there are other considerations. Between now and your foal's first saddling, he's got to learn to stand for the vet, to be haltered, to respect our space, to be led from here to there – the list goes on. Your job then, is to shepherd your foal for the next couple of years. You'll steer negative behavior into something positive, you'll quash poor habits, you'll set boundaries for the life of your horse.

This book will be broken into five days or segments. Don't take the word "days" super-literally, as you should take each section at a rate that works for you and your colt. You might move through this material (initially at least) in one business week, but the teachings are more meant to be absorbed, to be ruminated and factored into your everyday interactions at the barn. You've got a bunch of time until you can first climb aboard, so relax and take things slowly. There's more than enough time to fix your foal, break him, and fix him again. Babies can be exasperating things, seemingly trained today and true hazards again tomorrow. When you're breaking an older horse to saddle, you could very well go from "My horse won't back up" today to "My horse backs like a champ" tomorrow. When you're dealing with a weanling, he may be frightened of you today – fine with you tomorrow – and scared again next week. Or maybe your vet shows up – and you find that your colt is horrified of white hats. It's an evolving process and when you think you're done, you'll find you ain't. They're youngsters with no rhyme or reason so you'll need the patience of Job or an oyster or maybe both. Stay consistent with your training and, like a human teen, your foal will mature, even out, and make you proud.

Throughout this course I'll be careful to call out certain elements that I believe to be super-important for you to understand, practice or simply remember. Here's our first: If you've got two babies in a pen, one can be easy to train, the other can be a nightmare. Or, both easy or both difficult. It's the luck of nature's draw. If you fly through this training, be careful to keep your ego in check because your next filly can be the devil's spawn. Conversely, if your baby "doesn't seem to get it," take heed: I was speaking once to a (human) mother of four who I believed (and still do) to be one of the all-time great moms. She said that when her first two kids were born they were little angels and that for several years she walked around saying to herself "This mothering thing is easy. What's with all the brats?" Then she had two more kids, each a pill and a challenge – and she learned quickly that mothering is relative, literally. I tell you this because I've already walked a mile in the shoes you'll be walking in. I've been there and I know what it feels like to spend a fortune having a horse created, (the stud fee, the vet fee, etc.), to have waited a year for it to be born, to brag to everybody about the great genes... only to have it exasperate me as I work to get it to lift a leg, to thoroughly embarrass me in front of the vet or to have it give me a look like "You can't make me. I hate you." Be patient when things don't go your way, smile and remind yourself there's plenty of time. They're just kids.

Note before we begin: I can't stress the following enough. Young horses can be damaged forever very easily. You've got to keep your aggression in check. They've got baby lungs, baby legs, baby necks and baby brains. They may weigh two or three or four hundred pounds, but they've got all the physical and mental maturity of your infant niece or nephew. This advice may be more appropriate for my male readers, but we'd all do well to remember that while an older horse can be worked to a sweat in the round pen, the legs and lungs of a young horse will simply not hold up to extended exercise. This is an important point: If you work a very young horse in the round pen, for instance, he'll run like a frightened deer – and you might be tempted to keep him going to make your point (whatever it is at that moment) but your baby is in survival mode, running out of fear and could very well be doing permanent damage to himself. That's damage you may not see today – but damage that will come back to haunt you in the future. To put a point on this, think of it this way: If you've got a young gelding, and three years from now you find that he's virtually crippled from "those days back in the round pen," what do you do with him then? Bluntly put, he's an expensive yard ornament for twenty-something years or he's dog food. So listen up and take heed.

Babies can be run into fences (breaking necks), pushed through fences (shredding themselves) and pushed to the point of exhaustion (damaging lungs and legs). Josh Lyons, in his terrific "Foal Handling" video, has an excellent piece of advice: "If you're working a young horse – and either of you is sweating – you're pushing too hard." Keep that in mind as you work through this material: If either of you breaks a sweat, back off. Take a break or work to get the horse calmed by calming your requests. Horses don't think in terms of win and lose – so give it a rest. If you have trouble keeping yourself checked back then make a point to only work the baby when another person, a person who doesn't take guff from you, is there. That person's job is as a referee, to order a siesta at critical moments. Or, set yourself a time limit of, let's say five minutes. Five minutes tick by, you get out, no matter what. Or, carry around a piece of paper that says "When I lose my temper, I screw up my horse." No kidding, babies can be a challenge. Do what it takes to keep yourself in control.

Okay, next critical point to understand: To para-phrase John Lyons, there are three rules when working your horse – and they're especially true here with your foal. Whatever training you're doing or intend to do, keep in mind that your efforts must: 1) Not be likely to get you hurt, 2) Not be likely to get the horse hurt and 3) Your colt must be calmer at the end of the training than at the beginning. You should underscore rule number three with a pencil, as you'll be surprised how often it comes into play. It's a terrific concept to keep in mind because you are completely wasting your time out there if the horse is more excited at the end of your training than at the beginning. Simply put, if he's agitated, he's not learning. You'll see that for yourself in short order – but it's also just plain common sense: You can't force it into their brains. The baby isn't absorbing the lesson if he's a nervous wreck. If you've got five minutes left to train and your horse is wigging out – be conscious of this and stop pushing so hard. Take things slower and really aim to have a calmer horse by the end of your session. 5... 4.... 3... 2... 1... calm. Promise yourself that when you work with your colt you'll be cognizant of the fact that you need to be keeping and creating an ever-calmer horse. If you see him growing agitated, tell yourself that you're not keeping things simple enough or that's he's not ready. (Note: This does not mean that if he ignores us, shrugs off his lessons or otherwise becomes rude that we're to "do what it takes to keep him calm." Rather, in those cases it's particularly important to discipline. Don't ever be a patsy. Earning and maintaining respect takes equal parts discipline, patience and understanding.)

"Expectations" and "When to begin training": There are basically three types of baby horse owners out there reading this: There's the charged-up owner who plans on spending buckets of time hanging out with the baby each and every day and they've got to start training before the newborn is towel-dried. There's also the type who's got no time but wants to cover the basics to keep the horse safe and safe to be around. Finally, there's the person who's a mix of the other two. It's fine to fall into any of these groups because, wanna hear something funny? In about two years, each of these people will be at about the same place with their horses as long as they're consistent in their training in the meantime. Let me explain...

In the same way that geldings are easier to teach than mares and mares are easier to teach than stallions, your young horse will get easier to train as he gets older. If you're the type to hang out 24/7 with your youngster, that's great – but it's important to manage your expectations. The typical un-weaned baby is scared of his own shadow while you'll find the older horse less timid (thus more focused) and simpler to advance. (Note: I said "simpler," not "simple.") They're babies and logic is often illusive. They'll learn – it just takes more time, more repetition, more patience. It's a balancing act: Do I have to spend the time to teach this today – or can I wait a few months and get it done in half the time? I'll make these numbers up for the point of illustration, but you'll get the point: Let's say it takes 3 hours to teach a 2-month old to come to us, it might take a yearling one half hour. Credit babies accordingly. If you'd like to desensitize a colt today, great, but be aware that it might be exponentially simpler to accomplish six months from now. Be aware during your training sessions that you're working with young brains that have trouble retaining information and if things seem to be falling flat, perhaps you should give the horse some time to mature.

Personally, I split my approach – working in small ways daily with the colt or filly who has yet to be weaned to desensitize it to my presence or to respect my body positioning, (e.g., petting whenever possible, desensitizing it to the feel of the lunge whip and consistently enforcing rules like "Don't turn your rump to me" and "Don't crowd me" by urging it away). Later, when the horse is a couple of months past weaning I amp it up (adding in actual training plans where we focus on leading, picking up feet, etc.) Waiting some time beyond weaning gives the babies time to naturally become a bit more dependent, respectful and focused on me as I feed and work around them daily. Plus, waiting till Mom horse is out of the picture negates stress she might have otherwise been put through (that is, borrowing and working with her baby).

A frequent question is "How much time should I spend training?" I typically answer (for an adult horse) "Twenty minutes training followed by a twenty-minute break followed by a second session of twenty minutes." (Never mind the horse, twenty minutes is about as long as the average human can stay focused.) For the younger horse, you may want to stick with about twenty minutes flat, maybe add another ten minutes or so if he stays focused and learning. Stick with the "no sweat" rule and you'll be fine for that period of time – and if you have any doubt whatsoever, have a conversation with your veterinarian. While the mind of an adult can be kept occupied for longer periods, you'll find that the younger horse just sort of burns out just as a human child. Once they're "gone" they're gone and you're not going to make much improvement. Work 2-5 times a week and adjust according to good old-fashioned common sense. Also, try to keep your working days "in a row." If you can only work three days a week, work three days straight rather than one on, one off. Horses tend to forget stuff on those off days and you want to spend the bulk of your time teaching, not re-teaching.

What we'll cover in this book: In Section I, Day One we'll begin gently taking charge as we begin to control the direction of the horse and his movements.

The light bulb over his head flickers for the first time as your youngster begins to realize that we call the shots. Day Two capitalizes on the gains we've made, taking things a step further by desensitizing our colts to our touch, our presence and objects such as the lunge whip, halter and lead rope. We'll continue building our foundation on Day Three when we teach the horse to drop his head, soften his neck and readily accept being haltered and having his ears touched. Day Four is all about leading, and finally Day Five will show us how to bathe our foals.

Section II contains several lessons suitable for horses of all ages (like picking up feet or what to do if your horse bites). You'll want to get started on these things early, however, because babies are especially prone to nip as they grow and begin to test boundaries – and you certainly don't want to "hope for the best" when the farrier first drives up. You might very well end up losing a finger – and a farrier.

Where to go after this book: As previously stated, this guide will show you what you need to teach your weanling while you're waiting for him to mature to the point of being broke to ride. It'll give you the tools you need to turn your colt or young filly into a safe, respectable and well-mannered member of the family. When time has passed and you're ready to "break to ride," you'll need to first pick up a guide that covers round penning in more detail. There's much to be learned in the round pen; you'll be glad you invested the time spent there. After the round pen, the next step would be to look for information specifically geared for green horses, one that expressly addresses "bridling," "first saddling" and "the first ride."

Day One: Look At Me

We begin with simple body control.

Looking at your little, three-foot-high, doe-like foal, you may not think that you're starting it to be ridden here today – but you are. All training – every contact you have with it, really – goes into making it a safer, better, more obliging horse to ride – whether the first day you step aboard is today, tomorrow or two years from now. Every interaction the two of you have either hands you the horse's respect – or steals it away. John Lyons says (because it's very true) that "You ride the horse you lead." Horses that pull you around by the lead rope are guaranteed to tug on the reins and horses that bully you with their shoulders are certain to ignore you as beneath respect and insignificant when riding. Your horse's foundation begins here and now then, in this most simple of simple lessons, as we begin to control his elemental movements, safely and from the ground.

Ideally, you'll do the following in a round pen. If you don't have access to one, round off the corners of the pen you'll use by placing something there like water barrels, a tied-off garbage can, boards, etc. Skip this step and you'll find that they repeatedly head to the corners, stick their heads in there and freeze rock solid, just daring you to get those kicking feet moving again. Alternatively, you can do everything you'll find described here with the horse attached to you via a lunge line or lasso. You'd have to contend with continually swapping the line in your hands and watch for tangles, but if you adapt as common sense dictates, it is very doable.

Your goal here is twofold: To show the foal you're calling the shots and to build his confidence. See the seeming paradox? "Respect me, but don't be scared of me." You gotta walk a thin line – push too hard and you'll chuck prior improvements. Keep this in mind when you think about breaking a broom over young Dobber for dodging the halter for the 40th time. Lucky for us, horses are inherently wired to hand over respect to another being that gets it to move without hurting it. Watch horses in the field and you'll see how the alpha mare can move the others with simple body language – and how she rarely if ever resorts to actual, physical violence. (The next time you see two horses meet for the first time, note how the dominant horse will move the other in a corkscrew pattern.) We'll take advantage of this natural programming, factoring it into our first sessions.

Take your colt to your pen. I usually get them there by leading another horse he'll follow in there first, (like its momma), then circling around and leading the leader-horse back out, shutting the door before the baby can exit. Alternatively, you can begin laying out some feed in the work area a few days prior to get the youngster in the habit of going in there on its own. (I have no problem using bribes at this early, early stage.)

Now I've got good news and bad news. If you've got a nervous horse, one that's just a real jack rabbit, he'll be super simple to teach here because we need movement to teach – and your Nervous Nellie has got plenty of that. That's the good news. The bad news is, he'll be a pill later when you work to desensitize him to spooky objects. Alternatively, if you've got a real calm, friendly horse, you'll have to really work to keep him moving here. He figures he's your buddy, he's not scared of you – and he'll prove a challenge to keep moving. That's your bad news. Your good news is, he'll be a dream to desensitize later.

If you've got the horse that's just plain jumpy and skittish, then I want you to do the following. (If your horse seems relatively calm, absolutely do not do the following. Instead, skip ahead four paragraphs.) Super-jumpy horse owners, I want you to spend at least three days dulling your horse's sensitivity to his owner. I'll explain: You've seen this phenomena many times: In the same way that we burn out our brakes or clutch by constantly riding them, some riders burn out their "whoas" by saying it over and over to a horse. Repeat it often enough to a horse that doesn't stop and it doesn't take long before that word means nothing. Same thing with riders who constantly pull on the reins – their pressure soon means nothing. They've desensitized the horse to their requests. You're about to do the same, to burn out a "cue" but with good reason.

What you'll do is to bring your horse to the round pen, take up your lariat or lunge whip and ask him to move by taking a step toward it or raising the whip. (If it takes much to get the horse moving, you don't have a candidate for this particular work, forget this and skip ahead.) The direction doesn't matter as long as it's the same direction for five minutes, followed by a turn back the other way for another five and so on. Your high-strung colt will probably take off at a lope or high-speed trot. The higher speed is okay for a moment or two – but we want to conserve the baby's legs, lungs and overall strength – plus, the point here is to make him understand that he should move at a speed we choose and to be comfortable around us as well. Slow the horse down to a walk by moving slowly toward one side of the pen by a few steps so that the horse has to approach you on his next revolution. Move just close enough to break his gait to a walk, then immediately back away. If he turns or stops, you got too close. Get him going back the original direction the best you can (stand behind his withers and wave at his rump) and work for a smooth, medium-speed, cadenced walk. Stay very calm and relaxed, almost bored.

It's important that you realize that if you put too much of a squeeze on the baby you can send him dangerously into the fence – so start off slowly and test the waters. Find out what it takes to get him walking, then to keep him walking rhythmically without stopping or turning back. If or when he stops to scratch himself, look at you, yawn, stretch or nibble grass, that's a sure sign he's calmer. This first day, we're fine with that. Pause a beat, then simply gesture or move toward his haunches, pressuring him to get moving again. Do what it takes to cause your horse to move at a WALK consistently around in one direction for five minutes. He speeds up too much, you put the squeeze on him to slow him; he stops or turns, you correct him. When you turn him back, I want you to do it quietly like you're bored, bored, bored. Do just this (that is, keep him moving at a consistent walk in the direction of your choice) for your first session (of twenty minutes).

Go back out the next day and get your colt moving again at a walk. You've got a horse that needs to be desensitized to your very presence, so that's what we're doing here. Begin following your colt around the pen, ever closer. Press him, moving closer up behind him till he picks up a trot – then immediately position yourself to slow him back to a walk. (You've got to push till he makes a mistake so that he can learn from that mistake.) Walk after him again, moving closer and closer, until you're eventually (maybe today, maybe tomorrow, maybe the next day) walking abreast, starting him if he stops or correcting his direction till he learns to stay at an even walk with you next to him. Do just this for five minutes, turn back the other direction for another five and repeat to make your twenty. Keep him moving fluidly today, being quicker to fix any halting you might have purposely overlooked yesterday.

If you're ready to advance the next day, get him walking his cadenced circle again – but this time stand in the center of the ring and begin waving your lariat or lunge whip around overhead (like you're bored, not like you're on fire). Don't make a lot of eye contact. If the horse speeds up, keep swinging your lariat or whip above your head lazily, but squeeze the horse (as practiced earlier) to slow down. Over the next few minutes, gradually add pressure: Pick up the speed at which you swing the whip. Half-heartedly slap the ground. Move closer to him, then back away, closer, then away. Now, I know, we've all seen trainers chasing horses around with chain saws – but weanlings tend to get scared and stay scared if pushed too hard, so save the crazy shenanigans for later in your horse's life. When the horse will consistently and calmly walk around the pen with his head low, almost bored as you whip the ground (at a nice, calm, steady pace), do all of this again at a trot (remember the no sweat rule – "don't work a baby till it sweats" – takes precedence). After a few days of this, your horse should be decidedly more calm and tuned into you. You're ready to move on.

Calm-horse owners, re-join us here.

While the round pen work you're doing in the coming days is low pressure and done in comparative slow motion, you'll still be mirroring to a great extent the training you would do with an older horse. Teach the lessons well today, and a year or so from now your follow-up round penning sessions will be more a refresher course than something altogether new for your horse. You'll be teaching it to deal with fear, to stop or stand or move off when cued, to lead, and so on – just as you would the older horse. Most importantly – and this is the point you need to remember – most importantly, you're instilling respect because respect is earned by causing the horse's feet to move when and how you want them to move – while your feet stay relatively still. The key being that you need to accomplish this without unduly scaring the horse, causing pain or bullying.

Note: Even though we're working to build a calmer horse here, if at any time he flips you the metaphorical bird by only half participating, instantly correct the sour attitude with a shout, clap of the hands or crack of the whip (on the rump if need be). A bad attitude is not to be tolerated. You won't destroy the respect you've built when you're consistent with your discipline. Rather, you'll preserve or even improve it.

Begin by asking your foal to move around the pen at a walk or trot, (not a lope, "pressure and release" with your body language as described previously to control their speed). Your horse is naturally adept at reading body language so you can say "go forward" by applying pressure "behind the withers." That means that you stare at his rump and gesture with your hand or walk toward that area or throw your lariat at it, etc. Conversely, pressuring him from in front of his withers will send him backwards or initiate a turn (through his shoulders, away from you). Get him moving around the pen, let's say to your left. Next, ask him to turn in toward you by stepping backwards while sidestepping to your left, left arm outstretched as if to "peel" the horse off the wall as it approaches. If he looks like he's going to turn outside, be quick to jump directly to your right and toward that hip of his, putting pressure to say "get going forward right away" and allow it to go another half-turn before trying again. Be quick on your fixes and this will be easy.

Following your successful inside turn, the horse should be traveling to your right. Take a few beats rest then ask for another turn to the inside, asking the horse to turn and circle again to your left. Outstretch your right arm to "peel" him to your left, sidestepping to your right (to cut him off) while stepping back (stepping back gives him time to adjust for the movement). Here it is again in a nutshell: Hold out your right arm, sidestep to the right while backing up. You may need to work at this with some foals, as their natural tendency at first is to turn out (as if to run away). If your foal continually turns out, you may be getting too close to the fence and cutting him off instead of "suggesting" an inside turn with your body language. If such is the case, try backing away while kissing and lightly waving your arms to get it to look at you, in effect "drawing" its movement toward you. Be super-patient and upbeat; keep the pressure up and keep the foal moving and guessing. Once they figure it out, it gets pretty easy and they'll soon be turning in when you make even the slightest move.

When the horse is turning consistently and obviously "gets it," get more turns more often. Allow him to go just a few steps before asking for your next inside turn. He travels a few steps, you turn him; he travels a few steps, you turn him and so on. You'll notice that there's a natural lag time during the horse's turn (usually in that moment when he's nearly facing you). That lag time grows as you repeatedly stop and start him because the horse naturally starts to wonder if you aren't going to stop it again in another beat or two. Take advantage of this and experiment till you can stop the horse perpendicular to the fence facing you. (Can you see the natural payoff to teaching a horse to "turn in" toward you? Picture the horse who tries to move off as you approach with the halter. Practice enough inside turns and you'll have a fix for that.) Each and every time you stop your horse like this, approach it, pet it, praise it. (Stroke it with the tip of your lunge whip if you still can't get close enough with your hands; consciously work over time to shorten the distance.) Make that round pen the calmest, most tranquil, place on Earth for a good thirty seconds or so and your horse will soon learn that it can stand relaxed near you.

Next, we need to begin demanding that the horse keeps two eyes on us when requested. Look at your horse, standing there as positioned, perpendicular to the fence. Ask him to look at you with both eyes by making a kissing sound, then raising your arms or calling to him if the kiss doesn't work. Pause and, in a beat or two, he'll look away. Kiss to bring both eyes back. (Don't settle for one – get both.) We want the kiss to eventually become our cue for the horse to turn and face us, so be careful to begin with that each time you ask for the two eyes. Should he ignore your request, try clapping your hands, slapping the sides of the round pen, or cracking your whip... do anything it takes to get those two eyes back on you.

When he'll keep those eyes on you for several beats (and understands "kiss means look at the human"), build on this by sidestepping slightly to your right or left, expecting the horse's neck to turn and his gaze to stay on you. When he looks away, kiss – but, again, do what it takes to bring those eyes back on you if he ignores that kiss. He might turn and walk or even run away. If that happens (and it will) use your inside turns to bring him back into position. If he tunes out completely and begins ignoring you, don't be afraid to wake him back up. You're better off sending him back around the pen a time or two than you are letting him stand there, ignoring your requests. (Allowing him to ignore you inches you progressively down the respect totem. I can't stress this enough: Do not let your horse ignore you. He gets one request (one "kiss") and if he ignores that, we back it up with a clap, a scream, a smack of the whip.)

We want the horse's feet to step toward us, so don't get all hung up on whether he's technically perpendicular to the fence after you've been working awhile, that's just a starting point. If he moves away from the fence, stepping toward you, so much the better. Take advantage of that, sidestepping slightly to your right or left to see if you can't bait the colt to follow you as you inch backwards. Practice "keeping the two eyes on you" while moving until you can walk the circumference of the pen in both directions, the horse consistently and smoothly turning to face you like the hands of a clock.

Next step: Walk up to within several feet of the front of your horse. Kiss (saying "pay attention to me, movement is now required") and back away from the horse. When he moves toward you, smoothly sidestep to your right and, in an arcing motion, step towards the horse's left hip. If you successfully keep his eyes on you as you do this, his hips will sidestep away from you. Keep the horse's hip moving until his back leg that's closest to you steps in front of and across the other. This step will cause the horse to move slightly forward. The moment the leg closest to you goes to move in front of the other, back up a few steps, drawing the horse to you. (Kiss there if you need to for extra encouragement.) If you think about this, you've successfully gotten the horse to move both toward you and away from you based solely on your body language. (His hips moved away, his entire body walked toward you.) Now, how cool is that?

Finally, work to move the hips not by "pulling the eyes toward you," but by motioning or simply walking toward his hips. Begin by concentrating on drawing the horse's eyes toward you as if magnetized; use this and your positioning (walk at the hips, wave your arms, etc.) to cause those hips to move away. Repeat this, gradually, changing your primary focus from "pulling the eyes" to "moving the hips." Practice until you can simply walk toward those hips, or motion toward them and they'll move away with just a slight request. Also, consciously work to refine your "kiss cue," practicing till the horse will obligingly turn to face you with that simple sound; you'll need that for tomorrow's ("Day Two's") session. If you've been careful to ask for movement with just one kiss before backing it up with a shout or whip snap only when necessary, he'll have learned this "kiss cue" well by now.

Note: I use the kiss cue to mean "move something," maybe it means "those hips," maybe it means "your shoulders." I rely on the horse to read my body language (and they've got a gift for it) to understand which I'd prefer. To underscore my intent, I tend to also gesture toward the hips with my arm or walk toward them in order to get them moving. Don't over think this; the cues or gestures you naturally and unconsciously make will work just fine as long as you're focused and stay consistent because it's the repetition that makes them mean something.

Congratulations! You've taken a big step in your foal's training! Now you can ask the horse to turn and face you for haltering, bridling, or grooming – and, for safety's sake, you've got a way to ask those danger-ous back legs to cross away. You've gained respect and you're far less likely to get mowed over, should he become startled because now he respects your space. You've also developed a way to ask the horse to stand near you, to be comfortable and to be still. (He's far less afraid – but not bomb proof, don't be fooled. We'll continue to reduce his fear tomorrow when we delve more fully into desensitizing.) Note that, now that you have the ability to move his hips away upon request, you need to be adamant with your colt: Don't allow him to stand facing away from you (when you ap-proach, as you're feeding, for instance). For one thing, it's just plain rude; it's dangerous for another. Being expected to face you also instills a healthy respect and that's our goal in these pages. Horses that are carefully and consistently schooled on their manners rarely turn into biters, kickers or worse.

End of Day One

Day Two

Sacking Out and Desensitizing

Things that scare your horse fall into different categories and each category demands a different training approach. On one hand, there's stuff the horse comes into contact with frequently, things that may very well actually touch its body. On the other, there's the spooky stuff that your horse will probably never ever actually touch – but it's scary just the same (things like a fluttering flag, a clapping audience if you show, a rattling garbage can, or jack rabbits that pop out of nowhere).

Before you ride your horse, of course, you'll want to deal with all types of fear – but here and now, with a youngster, our priority will be to desensitize it to everyday objects that it comes into contact with – like brushes and clippers and our hands – in order to make it safer in everyday handling for us, our farrier, and vet – hence, our focus on what old timers refer to as "sacking out" here today.

(As your horse matures, you'll want to learn and practice an exercise John Lyons calls "Spook In Place" in order to condition your horse to deal with the unexpected, the flags in the arena, the garbage that blows across the trail, or the barking dog lunging from nowhere. It's an exercise designed specifically to condition your horse to keep its feet in one place – and your rear in the saddle – when these kinds of things happen.)

A quick note about sensitizing and desensitizing: There are times with every horse when you want to be sensitizing it to something and there are also times when you want to be purposely desensitizing. You want to "desensitize" your horse to the sound of the clippers running across its ears, but "sensitize" it to your leg pressure. You want to "desensitize" your horse to the touch of a blanket, fly spray, or inadvertent brush of your leg – but "sensitize" that same horse to pressure on the lead line, the crack of your lunge whip, kiss cue, or even your body posture. Here's how it works and what you need to remember: You sensitize a horse to something if you take the scary object away when the horse's legs are moving. You teach it that the scary thing disappears when it runs away. The opposite is also true. You desensitize when you take the scary thing away only when the horse is standing still. So, logically, you can sensitize your horse to pressure on the reins, but you can also desensitize your horse to pressure on the reins. You can sensitize your horse to the crack of the whip – or you can keep cracking it again and again and again while the horse is running and running and running... and thus desensitize the horse to the crack of the whip.

I'll say this again because it's hugely important and you don't want to be sharpening when you want dull and vice-versa: If you want your horse to become accustomed to something (desensitized), continue the stimulus until the horse stops moving (and then even afterward); if you want it to become sensitized remove the stimulus the instant the horse moves. See the difference? It's in the timing, it's **when** you stop doing what you're doing. We'll use this understanding, then, as we move forward, progressively "dulling" our horse to various objects.

To sack out your horse, tour your barn and surroundings, picking up buckets of objects, objects that range on the scariness scale from "probably not scary" to "guaranteed to scare." A hoof pick is probably not going to scare your horse, a crinkly-sounding plastic bag probably will. Be sure to grab the obvious like a brush, feed bucket, saddle blanket, lariat, lunge whip, bell boots, halter, lead rope, and bridle – but you should also get creative, placing a rock or two in a coffee can, tying two horseshoes together and so on. You'll need dozens of objects, keeping in mind that the more steps you put into this, the easier it'll be later when it comes time to put the halter on, or blanket, bathe or clip the horse. Look over the stuff you've accumulated and mentally arrange them from least to most scary.

A note to the wise: As I mentioned in yesterday's installment, babies can get scared and stay scared if you push them too hard. The work we're doing here should never reach the more robust pressures that we might subject an adult to. Working up to "most scary" involves something like wafting a saddle blanket or pad about and moving it around on the horse's back. It does not entail shooting off a pistol while revving up a chain saw and cracking a bullwhip. I push older horses pretty hard in an effort to "bomb proof" them and keep a rider safer; but your foal's brain will shoot to overload and stay there. So, relax. You'll have plenty of time to accustom your horse to nuttiness later in his life.

Before using the objects you've collected, let's add a step. Maybe our baby is feeling especially cantankerous today and if he is, we want to know that fact now rather than later because if he's over-the-top wired it can be dangerous for both of us. Or, maybe we've never seen this horse before and don't want to chance that it's a little extra sensitive and later we find that we pushed too hard, too fast. Or, maybe this horse just seems to look, I dunno, tense. (Here are some clues: Are you seeing the "whites of his eyes"? Is he standing there, rigid, head and neck raised, back bowed, his feet planted? Tense!) In the interest of safety, grab your lunge whip (you know, the kind that's rigid for about four feet before attaching to several more feet of line). If you've got one of those carrot sticks promoted by some of the big and famous trainers, you can use that, too. I like beginning with a lunge whip or carrot stick because it gives me the ability to test out the waters from a safe distance.

Station your foal in the round pen and ask him to face you. Now, the object of this game (here now with the lunge whip and later with your bucket of objects) is to bring the horse's emotions up a little, then lower them before he moves off. Raise and lower, raise and lower, asking the horse to cope with a bit more pressure with each repetition just as if weight-training a muscle. If he runs away, you lose points. Try less pressure next time, maybe a less-threatening angle or different body part. Your goal is to find a spot that gets a little rise out of him (a slightly raised head, a slight stiffening, etc.), then calm him back to zero. Raising his emotions slightly and calming him back down wins you a point. (If he does move off, simply reposition him facing you as previously practiced and start again.)

With the "rope part" of the lunge whip or carrot stick held up by your fingers to keep it from hanging loose, reach toward the foal and stroke his withers or the point of his shoulder once or twice then lower the lunge whip, smile broadly and say something nice. (You could begin with the horse's head, but I've found them to be more accepting of a touch to the withers or shoulder.) You may very well need to keep your contact to about a thousandth of a second, should the horse repeatedly move off. But that's okay, that's a start. Repeat this and sooner rather than later, your foal will begin to realize "Oh, that's all you wanted? No problem." He still won't trust you as far as he can throw you, but he'll soon let you dab his shoulders with the lunge whip if you simply stay with it.

Can't even get the whip to the horse? Back away and lightly smack the whip on the ground, snaking it about, toward the horse but back away before he can move off. If he does move away, keep moving the whip with the same intensity until the horse stops moving, then start again. (If he moves off and you stop your twirling, you're sensitizing him to the whip as described earlier – which is the opposite of what we want to accomplish.) Build on this till you can raise the whip to his shoulder and finally touch him with it, however briefly. In other words, "Start where you can." With more timid or younger horses, you may have only a second or two – and at some distance – before he moves off. If this is the case, start with a millisecond, build from there.

Practice this "advance/retreat" maneuver several billion times. Raise the whip, scratch the horse's back for 15 seconds, lower the whip and say something positive. One thing I like to do to break up the repetition is to occasionally simply turn my back on the colt and walk to the opposite side of the arena where I'll just hang out for thirty seconds or so. Horses are naturally curious and this can often pique their curiosity and cause them to become more "into" you. It mixes things up, can break up a good stalemate, and helps to keep the horse interested in you. (And it certainly reduces any threat he or she might feel.)

When the horse is thoroughly bored with his back being scratched, move your attentions to his neck. Then under his neck, down his front leg, over the length of his back, his belly and finally his back legs. Each time begin by rubbing something you've already worked on before moving to the new area. For instance, if he's okay with his shoulder being scratched, start there before trying his neck for the first time. This may initially take several sessions, but once they get the hang of this, they'll park out and just hang out, bored.

Ideally, you'll rub every spot for a count of 15, then lower your whip, take a few seconds breather, then repeat. You'll want to actively hunt the goosey spots (like between those back legs, under the tail, his ears, etc.) and concentrate on those until they no longer get a rise out of your horse. Trust me, you want to find those goosey spots and deal with them right now, here and today. Tell yourself that you'll get a hundred bucks for every goosey spot you can find and eradicate.

This is especially important with the horse's head: Head shyness is all too rampant and often grows worse as the horse grows older. Considering how difficult it is to do basic, necessary stuff (like haltering, bridling, blanketing, clipping, or worming your horse) when it's head shy – all foal owners need to take the time it takes – today – to get their horses over any sort of issues they may have. Promise yourself right now that you will work with your colt till those lips can be handled, the eyes and forehead rubbed, and the ears can be flipped, held, petted and otherwise humanely manhandled without objection. Not only are head-shy horses dangerous and irritating, but they also label you as somebody who shouldn't own a horse. A green horn. A schlub. I'm half-convinced that horses see the ability to avoid having their ears touched as a test: "Is this owner of mine a dufus or what?"

Being careful to stay clear of those kicking feet, set about testing out those ears. Some babies simply won't care, others would rather die than have an ear bent forward. Dab as near to the ear as you can actually touch, rub, then drop your whip as before and pet with your hands the parts of the horse you can safely pet. (Go easy, touch or stroke lightly; they're his ears after all.) If you can move one ear, great, flip it back and forth and check it off your list. To deal with an ear that doesn't want to be touched, the idea is "touch it so quickly" that the horse doesn't even have time to move off. Stay with it, keep calling him back if you need to, and gradually slow down the passes of your whip till he'll stand for more and more. If he gets irritated by this, tough beans. Do it some more. Who's paying the bills around here? This is one battle of wills you must win... if you ever want to get the bridle over his head. Stick with this until you can flip his ears back and forth like light switches, until you can wrap the rope part of the whip around his ears lightly and until he stands there calmly as you do so. If he looks irritated, keep doing it till he becomes more accommodating. Later, when we begin using our hands to desensitize, make sure that you stick with it till you can squeeze (lightly) the base of his ears and also brush the tiny hairs within the ear back and forth – two tests he'll need to pass in the future, like when it comes time to bring out the clippers.

(Note: If there is a real chance that your horse is suffering from painful bug bites in its ears, skip that area for a week or two and circle back. In the meantime, stand safely at the horse's shoulder and spray the ears with a high-quality fly spray. If your horse is not yet "used to" such a thing, fill an empty spray bottle with tap water and desensitize it with that before wasting your expensive spray. Give it some time, then come back and desensitize the horse's ears. Once they can be handled, apply a roll-on fly repellent sold for just such a thing.)

Moving on, you'll use the "rope part" of your whip to desensitize the horse's back legs. Bring the whip aside then smoothly toward the back legs, causing the rope to wrap around or between the legs. Give the rope a few tugs and do whatever wacky thing you can think of to get the horse accustomed to being touched there. Keep in mind that horses that kick back at objects that unexpectedly touch their feet are telling you that they'd do the same to your head if you fell off. Trust me, you'll want to spend quality time desensitizing those back legs.

You might be tempted to hold the foal in place should he try to move off or pitch his head away. Don't do it. Chasing after the baby will serve as proof to him that you're not to be trusted. Trying to hold him in place will at best antagonize your horse, at worst it'll get you kicked. If he moves off bring him back with an inside turn or kiss. This can be tedious and will be sort of a pain for you, but in the end he will have learned the material better if he's not forced and comes to the conclusions on his own. Each time he takes his head away, ask with a kiss or a light waving motion to have him bring his head back to you. Get used to doing this; you'll have to "bring him back to you" several trillion times. (By the same token, if you get the feeling that the horse is just playing you, that he's not trying or bored with you, don't be afraid to clap your hands or do something else to wake him up. Send him back around the pen a time or two at a jog to bring back his focus and create energy.)

It wouldn't be unheard of for the horse to signal that he's tired of you sometime during today's prescribed exercise by trying to give you a good kick. Until recently, his days consisted of lying about, suckling, pooping and switching at flies. Now you're putting him to work! Be careful to stand clear (near the point of his shoulder, slightly off to the side). If he kicks (or even thinks about it as signaled by a threatening raise of a hind leg) scream your bloody head off and chase him away. Let him know immediately and in no uncertain terms that this is not acceptable behavior. (Same goes for nips.) He'll run around a bit, but you just need to bring him back to you as you've been practicing and begin again.

Finally, you'll take up your "bucket of scary things" and use them to run through the same process you just did with the whip. Your hands will be the least scary objects, so begin by petting your horse where you can and build on that. Pet, retreat, relax, repeat, as described above. Be careful to always begin with an area where the horse stands relaxed (maybe his back, maybe his shoulders) and to move from there to the new spot (like his back legs). Remember to stand safely at the point of his shoulder when practical. (And when standing near, don't drop your "scary object" over to the other side of his back if it might scare him into you.) Don't forget to thoroughly desensitize those ears and lips.

When the horse will stand there, his head dropped and neck relaxed, a soft and bored look in his eyes, you can move on to the next object, like your hoof pick.

(Horses show that they're comfortable by cocking a back leg in a relaxed manner, licking their lips, dropping their heads, and/or allowing their eyelids to droop. If a horse is uptight, you'll notice tense muscles, a raised head, the whites of it's eyes, and a rock-solid, planted-like-a-tree posture.) Take up your hoof pick next then and rub it all over the horse till he's bored silly. A bored horse is your cue to move to the next-scariest object on your list and repeat the process. Remember, the more objects you add in, the easier your "most scary object" will eventually be. Also note that when you work with objects that can be folded (for instance, towels, plastic bags, or saddle pads), start with them folded and work like that till the horse stands relaxed before opening the object progressively, repeating the steps as necessary. But also, make it a point to open or unfold the object as you approach the horse. Opening it as you approach gives you another opportunity to "scare" the horse because you're holding something that's morphing, that's actually growing larger in the horse's eyes. Repeat this entire process until you can swab his entire body with your most scary object (like a crinkly plastic 50-pound feed bag).

Build your investment in your horse by working everyday to broaden your baby's acceptance to new stimuli. Be creative in your approach and remain vigilant. Don't put yourself in dangerous positions (between two youngsters who might become startled, for instance); always ask for the tail to turn away from you when you're near (to feed, for example, as outlined in yesterday's segment) and be sure to harness good old common sense.

End of Day Two

Day Three

Halter-training Your Foal

If you've done a proper job of sacking out your baby (and this means desensitizing your foal on both sides of its body, in every nook and cranny, and you can't find another "goosy spot" for a million bucks) then we're ready for the halter.

Here in Day Three we'll use "halter training" as an excuse to better understand – and deal with – our youngster's many moods. We'll get that halter put on – but along the way, we'll load in additional training, training designed to improve your baby's overall attitude toward you and the tasks you ask it to perform.

We have four things to accomplish now, four things to check off our list before continuing on to tomorrow's material. 1) I want you to be able to honestly say that you see and understand when your baby is in an agreeable mood, ready for training – versus when it's radiating warning signals that it's inordinately frightened, stressed, or tense (and know what to do to calm it down). 2) You need to understand the difference between a horse that's trying and one that's not. 3) You should be able to put the halter on and take it back off, including past those ears, while your horse's head stays down and he remains calm and agreeable. 4) Your horse must coolly stand after you've taken the halter off until you release him. By the end of the day, your response to each of these statements must be "Yes, got it." If it's "Kind of" you are not allowed to move on. (I'll know you cheated if you call me or another pro trainer several years now and offer to pay us big money to come fix one of these issues.)

First, I need you to objectively understand whether your horse is "cool with things" and to consistently diagnose this from now on when you're working together. You've been handling your baby for some time now and should have enough under your belt to quickly spot some issues I'll describe. It always amazes me as I travel from clinic to clinic and find folks (here in the States, in Germany, the Czech Republic, everywhere) who are oblivious to the seething cauldron of emotions their horses have become. The horses "feelings" have been ignored – leading to sometimes explosive issues – and the owner wonders where it all came from. Duh. Tense horses aren't learning and are dangerous to boot.

This is a simple thing really, a matter of you looking over your horse and taking stock of his mood. Bring your foal out to your training area and let him wander. Lean back against a fence and look him over. Is he stiffly running around with his head high in the air, looking out of the ring, ignoring you and calling to his buddies? Tense. When he turns to you, can you see the whites of his eyes? Scary tense. When you move around him, (today, yesterday, tomorrow), does he stand unnaturally rock solid, like a fainting goat, his feet planted, the muscles in his neck and back taut, maybe even shaking? An accident looking for a place to happen tense. Note these things when you work your colt. Realize that the horse that's running around like a lunatic isn't learning jack, nor is the one standing there too petrified to move. If at this stage your horse is still a nervous wreck when you turn him out – a real scared rabbit – go back and repeat the work set out in Day One, the part where you desensitized it to your "nearness" in the round pen. You haven't quite nailed that.

If the horse isn't running out of panic, but more or less because he's ignoring you entirely, basically blowing off your very presence, then simply ask for a series of inside turns by using your body positioning to turn him toward the center of the pen as he circles around toward you. Keep it turning in over and over until it slows down and keeps its eyes on you. Increase the frequency of the turning (and consciously adjust your own positioning) until the horse comes to a halt.

If you're working near him and you sense him standing as rigid as Frankenstein, back away and ask him to move about before asking him to turn back to you. Get lots of forward, flowing movement and turns. Never work around a frozen horse (of any age) – their next move could be right over you. Ask them to move around, perhaps take things slower and then ask again. (Literally turning your back and walking to the other side of the pen and taking a moment's break will also serve to calm his fears and somewhat shove him back into neutral.) Be calm yourself and request repeated inside turns to bring his emotions down (not to tire, but to create focus). That's when the learning begins.

Or – by contrast – maybe when you turned him loose he quickly settled down and just sort of meandered about.... Did he drop his head, sigh, nibble grass and altogether look bored by his situation? Did he wander over to you and sniff, maybe make a chewing sound? Or mouth your lunge whip? Excellent. All good signs. That's the way you want your horse to look while you're working with him. Not actually bored, of course, but content.

So then we move to Item Two on our list: Diagnosing horses that are putting in an effort versus those that are not. Quality training involves your ability to understand that you might be pushing your horse too fast. He's trying, he's just not getting it. But, it also requires that you understand when you're being played for a fool.

We've all seen riders with bratty horses making one excuse after another for their situation. "He only bites when he's tired." "He won't get in white trailers; his mother was killed in a white trailer." Spare me. The horse gets his way – and he gets worse every day. Y'know, the typical inmate doesn't "just end up in" prison. He's been ignoring boundaries for years. Same goes for difficult horses – they've been allowed to slide downward for quite some time. You have the opportunity now to start your baby out on a path that'll lead to many years of quality time on the trail, chasing cows or taking blue ribbons. You just have to establish a zero tolerance policy to bad behavior; give the horse credit when he tries, and discipline when it's deserved.

The horse described above that's running around the round pen, calling to his buddies and ignoring you is not only tense – he's also lost to any training you might think you're doing. You'll want to ask for those inside turns not only to channel his energy (and therefore calm him) – but also to cause him to focus on you. The two results go hand in hand. Be aware as you ask for these turns, however, of a subtle change: At some point, the horse will begin to tune in to you as evidenced by him keeping two eyes on you or cocking his ears toward you or by completing his turns fluidly or by looking at you after the turn as if to say "What's next?" It's very, very, very important that you are aware of this and always, always, always know which horse (Jekyll or Hyde) you're looking at at any particular moment.

Start being very much aware of when your horse is trying and when he's not. Know that "trying" might include him making a mistake or series of mistakes over and over for days. Mistakes are great. Mistakes show us the horse is trying and they show the horse what not to do. Blundering upon the answer doesn't signal an understanding. Be happy he's making mistakes; they signal that he's running through a learning process. Horses (babies, adults, all of them) that are trying deserve tons of patience and all the time in the world to figure something out. If I ask my colt for an inside turn and he repeatedly turns outside instead, I'll ask myself if it's due to something I'm doing that might be improved, maybe my body language. Can I improve my communication and make something clearer. Is it me? Or is he just being a turd? If I sense a lack of try or overt rudeness, as evidenced by him ignoring me and whinnying to his buddies or by a marked laziness or by a "Who do you think you are?" look, I'll amp things up and make him work harder.

With an older horse I'll speed the sucker up, maybe move him around till his lungs say to his brain "Hey, figure something out!" But don't try that with a youngster. That is absolutely a no-no. With a foal (remembering the "If it's sweating, you're pushing too hard" rule), our recourse is more limited. Use your voice or clap your hands, try snapping the whip or running at him to demand an awakening of sorts. If he'll only move off at a lackadaisical speed as if blowing you a raspberry, then by all means, snap him in the rear with the whip. But, if you've been quick to fix his mistakes, his overall respect for you should stay strong. Even when he's trying his heart out be careful to not allow him to "get sloppy" through his repetitions (his inside turns, for instance). Allowing him to just "go through the motions" will gradually eat away at the respect he has for you. Don't nag and don't drag things out. Keep things snappy and interesting.

Okay, with you and the colt there in the pen, let's tackle number 3 on our list of today's goals: Let's get the horse haltered. Begin by rubbing your foal stem to stern with the lead rope balled up in your hand. Rub his head and ears with it. If he's okay with that, if he stands there calmly, then progress by rubbing the horse all over with the lead rope folded in half. Droop it over his ears and allow it to catch there, pulling his ears forward and back. Wrap the lead around his neck and tug it back off. Bring it with a swing to wrap around his torso, back legs, neck and head. Keeping yourself there at the point of his shoulder, use both hands to bring the lead back and forth several dozen times past his eyes. Try moving faster. Make a little noise. Get creative and do everything from both sides. Stay vigilant because you'll always be surprised at the strange combinations of movements that will frighten your horse when you wouldn't have expected it.

Now let's consciously desensitize the horse to being touched by something on the opposite side from which we're standing. He sees us on his left side, for instance, and expects to be touched there – but dropping our arm across to his right side and unexpectedly brushing him could cause him to jump away from our hand and right over us. Don't become a statistic, as they say, so pay attention here: Stand slightly to the side at his shoulder and throw the lead rope across his back, focusing on the pressure caused on his "off side" as you draw the rope back. Pitch the lead repeatedly back and forth across his withers at various lengths. Pat or rub the horse down along the side on which you're standing, down along where a cinch would fit then reach under his belly with your whip (or foot, whatever's handy) to snag and pull the lead rope back to you (under his belly) so that it now wraps completely around his barrel. Alternately tighten and loosen the rope, accustoming him to being touched through all of his 360 degrees. (This also accustoms him to the feel of the cinch.) Saw the rope, bringing it to the front and back of the horse until he's comfortable with that. You can and should do something similar between both front and back legs as well.

  Next pet him across his top line and gradually pet your way across his spine and down his opposite side. Pat him there. Pet the devil out of his ears, scratch under his chin, make a game out of playing "Peekaboo" covering his eyes one at a time, then both together. Get really creative. When or if you find resistance, keep petting (or waving or scratching, etc.) for 15 seconds or until the horse calms down, whichever comes first. Take the time to dull him to movement, fast and slow, on all sides of his head, paying particular attention to his ears and eyes. All of this work on his off side is necessary because in a few minutes you'll want to reach across to bring the halter around – and if you've skipped this step, your hand running past his eye can become an issue. As with our previous work, if the horse steps away just kiss to bring him back; remain nonchalant; don't give chase with your hand or body.

In the end, actually getting your colt haltered is a piece of cake. By now he should be so used to hands and various objects coming at him and rubbing him, that a simple halter is no big deal (a relief, maybe). Take your halter, remove the lead rope to simplify things, ball the halter up in your hands and... you guessed it, desensitize the horse about the head and neck. When he's relaxed, unfold it and do the same thing again, making sure to droop it purposefully over his ears, up and around his muzzle, etcetera. Mock the same motions you'd go through to actually place the halter over his head, reaching around his head, bringing the halter here and there... and finally just put the darn thing on him. (Don't be all ginger about it. Prey animals know when you're sneaking around and that really sets off alarms.) Pause and pet a moment or two, then unbuckle the halter, slide it up and down his snout several dozen times and finally remove it altogether. Put the halter on and take it back off till he's okay with the procedure, then do everything again – but walk away from him then back to him with each repetition. Keep things varied and interesting. You may be surprised how startled they can become when approached from different angles. Be prepared to repeat some amount of this desensitizing to the halter each day for several days until it becomes routine for the baby. Check off today's box three – you've haltered your foal.

Which brings us to the fourth thing on our check list: Teach the horse to move off politely after the halter comes off and only after being excused by us. This is just a matter of calling the horse back to us (with our kiss cue), should he pull away or amble off rudely or selfishly when the halter is removed (at which point you can put the halter back on and off until the attitude improves). If you instill this habit of standing politely within the youngster, and remain consistently adamant, he'll always be good about this. The "trick" I use to enforce this habit is a simple one: I just pet the horse briefly (between his ears, maybe a scratch of the withers) each and every time I remove the halter, spending 5-20 seconds of "quality time." My horses have learned through repetition that their signal that we're through is me turning my back on them – and that that comes only after a moment or two of petting. They know without a doubt that I'll just call them back and annoy them further if they move off prematurely.

Horses that run off are dissing you, telling you in no uncertain terms that you are not the boss of them. Be rock steady in your discipline as outlined in this book, and you'll be shocked at how easy it is to keep a polite horse. To check this off your list as truly accomplished, you must circle with a pencil or say out loud the following: "I will never allow my horse to pull away impolitely as I undo the halter. If he does, I'll call him back, re-halter him, scratch him till we're both bored, then try the whole thing again. Even if it's three in the morning."

(If your horse – young or old – has already developed the habit of charging off dangerously as you unbuckle the halter, then do the following: With your horse haltered, hold one end of the lead line and deliberately ask it to move away from you. Allow it to travel a few feet, then bring it to a stop and ask it to turn back toward you by adding pressure to the lead line. Don't "pull" the horse back toward you, simply add pressure to the line and wait for the horse to hit the end of it. Practice this until the horse starts keeping an eye on you as it moves off because it reckons that you're seconds away from asking it to turn back again. Repeat the sequence then, asking your horse to travel even farther away. Allow it to hit the end of the lead and turn back as previously practiced and until the horse once again learns to keep an eye on you. Note that if you're working with a baby, the bones and muscles in their necks are immature. Do not abruptly "jerk" their heads back to stop them. Instead, take a moment or two to gradually add pressure to the lead line in order to ask the foal to turn back, like a car brake gradually being applied.)

End of Day Three

Day Four: Leading the Colt

Your foal's ground manners today correspond directly to his quality as a riding horse tomorrow. (If he drags on the lead now, he'll ignore your reins entirely later.)

Today we'll teach your foal to lead properly, a necessary basic, of course – but also an excellent opportunity to introduce the number one concept in all of horse training: "Give to pressure." Pick up the reins and ask the horse to turn, stop, back, or drop its head... he's giving to the bit, and therefore to pressure. When he moves away from our leg bumps, picks up a hoof to have it picked, leads willingly... with all of these things, he's giving to pressure. If he wasn't, he'd be tugging on the reins to nibble grass, pulling back as he's tied, dragging behind while being lead, or barreling ahead ignoring our request to stop. Training is first and foremost about "giving to pressure."

"Giving to pressure" has to consciously be taught because horses come to us pre-programmed by nature to resist applied pressure – just like we humans naturally resist pressure put upon us. To prove it, walk up to any person and hold your palm toward them. Just look at them and they'll respond by putting their palm against yours. If you then push, 999 out of 1000 people will push back. Why? Who knows, but your horse thinks the same way. "Giving in" is not a normal reaction and far from instinctual so we'll begin today to re-wire your colt, working to make "giving" a first response.

Note: Typically, of course, horses are on our right side when we lead them and all the training described here will assume that you're working with your horse in that same traditional position. However, at some point in the not-too-distant future, you should reverse the things you learn here and teach your horse to lead from both sides.

With your horse haltered, and a lunge line attached to the ring of the halter, stand on his left side and grab the line several inches below his head. Apply light pressure toward your body; let's say two pounds worth. We want the colt to either turn his head slightly or relax his neck, whichever comes first. Drop the line the instant you feel even the slightest relaxation from the horse. If thirty seconds goes by with nothing, try adding just a little more pressure or maybe another angle, more "up," more to the side, more cattywampus. If still nothing, it's a good guess you're looking for too much. When you first begin, he may tip his head by just a hair or relax for but a millisecond. Release on the smallest of small gives here and build from there. Release if you think he's **even thinking** of giving. Practice until these simple gives happen effortlessly. If you ask him to bring his head to the side and he responds by swinging his hips around (a typical response), just drop your pressure entirely and try again with a less pressure and slower movements.

For the next few hours worth of training, be aware of how your horse turns its body. How it turns toward you tells you what's happening in that brain and, hence, what point you're at in your training. It's closely related to yesterday's "Is he relaxed or not" lesson and something to start being on the lookout for. If your horse turns toward you stiffly by swinging its hips across, keeping his neck straight, and front feet planted, that marks a certain amount of resistance or nervousness – and this is what you will see when you begin your training. On the other hand, when the horse turns toward you by walking forward through its shoulders, bending through its neck and body like a giant snake, then you've got a good sign that the horse is comfortable with you and working with you. It indicates that your training is taking hold.

After your horse has been introduced to giving to pressure, we're ready to move on. Position it near the wall of your pen, stand back a good ten feet or so, and ask it to walk ahead, circling to the left. You should stay equi-distant behind the foal as it walks, by roughly 10 feet. (Be sure to stay a full "horse and a half" length behind if you feel that getting kicked is even a remote possibility.)

Note: You must develop the ability to move your horse away on cue. By now the horse will have begun to understand that being near you oftentimes means he gets to chill out so he may be slow to move off now; he might keep turning back toward you, he might simply stand there. However, allowing your horse to ignore your cue to put distance between the two of you creates a very dangerous situation. It is not cute. A horse that thinks it can pick and choose which of your requests it'll honor is a very dangerous animal, one that's far more likely to step right over you or your neighbor's 3 year-old child should it become startled, angry, or otherwise pressed. (And, yes, I'm talking about that sweet old horse who'd never hurt a fly.) When you cue the horse to move off and away from you, be quick with a motivational snap of the whip (in the air or to the rump when necessary) to back up your request and prove that your bark has bite. You won't destroy any bond you've created; you'll be fostering necessary respect. If you can call your horse to come to you, but not send him back away, you've only got half the puzzle.

Ask the horse to meander around the circumference of the pen. You want him moving a moment or two before you do anything further because you need to instill the concept that movement is part of this work. You want to encourage fluid movement, not a "stop-start-stop-start," sticky motion. When he's moving out nicely, apply light pressure to the lunge line and wait for the horse to stop. The moment he does, drop your line and praise him. Practice this a few times. If he tries to approach you, put him back in position.

The next step is to get him moving again, still circling to the left, but this time, allow him to go a few feet, then pick up the line, ask for him to tip his head ("giving to the line") – and insist that he keep moving. He'll want to stop because that is what's been handing him a release from our pressure until now, but you need to push him to walk on (with a wave of your hands, a flick of your whip, maybe a smack of the coiled lasso on your leg). If you've completed the initial work (where you simply stood there and took the slack out of the line till he looked at you), this will not be all that new a concept for the foal.

When the horse will calmly move off ahead of you with his head slightly cocked (only very slightly, just look for a relaxed neck and an inch or two of bend), gradually begin walking closer and closer to him. It won't be long before the two of you are walking abreast. He might feel a little intimidated at first and reticent to move ahead when you draw up close, but take it easy, keep coaxing, and he'll soon grow accustomed to you being there. Should he slow down, simply turn back and stare at that hip to get it moving again, maybe swishing the end of the lead toward his rump for a little extra "oomph." (If it slows down repeatedly, position yourself farther back along the horse's body as you walk – so instead of his neck being at your elbow, his ribs or even rump might be. Move into a "normal" leading position as you can.)

As you're walking there alongside the horse, very gradually turn in toward the center (in a wide arc to your left if you've been walking a circle to the left). If the horse dutifully keeps the slack in the rope, if he "gives to it" as he's been taught, he'll follow alongside you. If he fails to turn, apply pressure to the lead, dropping it as you feel him soften and turn. "Flow" around the pen with no particular direction in mind; just keep the horse moving and changing directions very gradually, adding pressure then releasing to encourage the horse to associate your movement with his.

Throughout today's assignment, you've got to ignore your desire to jerk on the lead line should the horse balk. It's tempting to try and pull the horse ahead – but pulling hard or rudely snapping the lead line simply causes the horse's head to shoot up and his body to become rigid. He doesn't learn anything (though everybody at the barn may learn you're in over your head). Anytime the horse lags back, the answer isn't "jerk, jerk," the answer is for you to get those hips moving; that's where the power comes from. Get the hips unstuck by tapping on the horse's rump with the end of your lead line or a dressage whip.

Anytime your training seems to stall out or your foal appears unduly nervous, return to a point in your training (even if it means a return to materials in Days One, Two or Three) and work from a point where he's comfortable. It's likely you need to take things slower. Unlike mature horses, it's sometimes easy to force or manhandle a baby – but forcing something doesn't necessarily equate to "lesson learned" and it can be dangerous now or later.

As you practice, concentrate on asking the horse to "work on less," meaning here that you want to consciously cause him to follow not your pull, but your body language. Challenge yourself to always keep some slack (an actual droop) in the lead line. (Easy to do if you keep turning to the hips to add drive, rather than pulling on the lead.) That droop will serve as your proof that your horse is learning to work off your body language and not being coerced.

When your horse will walk easily alongside you, walk the circumference of the pen, again circling to your left. After a few beats, find an opportunity to walk a bit faster and then turn to your right abruptly – yet smoothly – and walk directly toward his head and neck, cutting him off and asking him to turn toward the fence. At first, your horse will either keep moving forward, cutting you off, or he'll stop entirely. When he does, just put it in your mind that you're asking for an "up-close" outside turn: On Day One, you asked your foal to turn in toward you and the center of the ring (you asked for an "inside turn"). Now, get an "outside" turn by positioning yourself in front of his withers and applying pressure through your body language to turn his shoulders **away** from you and the center of the pen. If need be, wave your arms toward his eye to move him off or tap him on the shoulder. You might also try positioning yourself away from your horse by a good ten or fifteen feet as you ask him to "turn out," gradually reducing the space between the two of you until he gets the idea. Get an "outside turn" from ten feet, then nine, eight, seven, etc.

To teach the horse to back, try one of the following: A) Walk along the fence and practice several outside turns. Three or four times in succession you'll pivot and walk toward the horse's neck, asking it to move away, toward the fence just as before. Put some energy into this and the fifth time turn more to the horse's chest and signal "back" with your motion, simultaneously applying slight backward pressure to the lead line. If he stalls out, get him moving forward immediately and try again. B) Move away from the fence and use pressure on the lead line to ask the horse to bring its nose toward its hip, forcing the hips to move away, causing the horse to pivot over his front shoulder. Before the hips come to a stop, apply pressure on the lead and divert his energy backwards or sideways and then backwards. If he stalls out, quickly get him moving in any direction, then ask those hips to move sideways and try for a back up once again. If you work at your timing and keep at this, you'll succeed, if only by accident. C) If you have one of those fiberglass carrot sticks, walk toward the chest of the horse swinging the stick left and right (parallel to the ground) at a medium tempo and allow it to smack the horse in the shoulder as you approach. You should swing it with an even pace like a metronome. The nice thing about using the stick is that the stick is objective – either the horse moved when he got within the length of that stick – or he did not. There's no second-guessing whether a smack is called for. It won't hurt the horse – but it will certainly startle it, sending a clear signal to "back away." Regardless of which method you use, once he gets the idea, it's a simple thing to teach the horse to back based on your body language.

Next, practice walking the fence line as previously practiced – but pick up your pace and ask the horse to begin trotting. Work to get your horse to the point where he'll immediately pick up the pace or slow down to match your quicker strides. Have fun with this and practice many stops and starts plus abrupt changes of direction and speed. (You'll soon find that when you simply lean forward, the horse will actually lean as well.) Anytime he moves beyond you, (which is likely if he becomes excited), execute a few sharp turns in quick succession and he'll learn how best to position himself. Really do take the time to teach this material at a faster pace; the precision and "flashiness" of your horse's movement will improve immeasurably.

When you're ready, leave the confines of the round pen and go explore. Your foal thinks the world consists of a stall or paddock so you'll want to carefully and methodically accustom your baby to all sorts of sights and smells. Remember to come at everything from both directions. It's easy to think they've seen something; they should be okay with it. But unfortunately, their right brain doesn't seem to ever pass info to the left brain. Make sure that all experiences are experienced from all angles. You want a calm, "worldly" horse when you trailer to the first show or roping, so get out there and spend some quality time together.

Note: Train where you can, not where you can't. If your horse wigs out at the sight of garbage cans or traffic, start 100 steps away from the scary object. Work him there on those things you've been practicing (giving to pressure, leading, turning to face you, desensitizing, etc.) until he calms down, then try 99 steps away. Keep edging in till those garbage cans are no longer a big deal. He won't forget them; he'll just learn to keep his focus on you. Be realistic in your expectations when out exploring. You've got years before he reaches something resembling mental maturity, so don't force things; don't ask for trouble. Typically, you should be able to get the horse well-trained to lead in about three sessions of forty minutes each.

End of Day Four

Day Five: Bathing Your Foal

Teach your foal to stand properly for a bath – but also see this as an opportunity to strengthen your position as leader in your herd of two.

Whether you plan on showing your horse in the arena, or to simply show him off to your friends, you'll sooner or later have to accustom him to taking a bath. I give my horses a shower (sans soap) any time it's warm and they work up a sweat. Besides helping to avoid nasty skin problems, it helps cool them down before I feed them. I can get them hosed and scraped off in a few minutes, so it's a no-brainer on an especially hot day. This is easy stuff. Time consuming maybe to teach, but no problem when taken step-by-step. Like many objects on this planet, the hose, sponge, wash rack, sweat scraper and even rushing water are all new to your foal – so your biggest challenge will be keeping your cool and not screaming things like "It's just water!"

Note that you can teach your foal to accept fly spray by following this method as well. Simply substitute the bottle for the hose. (Fill it with water initially; you don't want to spend eight trillion dollars on expensive fly spray, nor would you want to cover your horse with 40 pounds of chemical residue.)

Note also: For now, don't tie your colt at the wash rack; he hasn't had that training yet. The bones in the neck of a young horse are easily damaged – causing him to pull back while tied is to be avoided.

While some horses will soon learn to actually like being hosed down or otherwise babied, others will at best tolerate it for the rest of their lives. Hey, I still don't eat tomatoes and no amount of being whacked will make them taste good – so I accept that we all have our differences. But.... if you've never trained a horse to bathe before or you're not sure how yours will accept a shot of water to the forehead, don't wait till the day of the show to try this out. Like trailer training, it's something you want to test at least the weekend before.

Wash racks are slippery places so the sacking out you've done beforehand needs to be rock solid. You want to avoid confrontation entirely so be quick to return to prior training when or if it becomes necessary. If, for instance, your foal simply refuses to allow his head to be showered, leave the wash rack altogether and spend more time sacking out his ears, eyes, and muzzle. You've practiced that already, but this time use more objects, maybe ones that make more noise or have a decidedly different feel to them. (Rustling wax paper, a length of rope that approximates the look and feel of a hose, a dripping sponge, etc.) If he's got issues with the hose touching his back feet, fall back and practice with your lunge whip or lariat, wrapping and unwrapping his legs. Teaching your youngster to stand calmly here is a piece of cake when you've taken the time to desensitize it as necessary.

If you have the luxury of picking your days (and hence the weather), do yourself a favor and choose a hot day. First, you won't have to worry about him staying wet and getting sick, second the cooling effect will help make him see the bathing rack as a pleasant place. (You should avoid cold days altogether.)

If your horse is unfamiliar with the wash rack, bring along a dressage whip in addition to your water bucket, sweat scraper, shampoo, conditioner, etc. The floors of most racks are simply poured cement and this new sensation can cause your foal to balk and refuse to even enter the area. Should the horse plant his front feet and refuse to approach, don't try forcing the issue. (Not only is that dangerous on a slick surface, it'll solidify his initial thought that bad things happen there.)

Instead, work on your "go forward" cue: Get as close as you can to the wash rack with the foal relaxed. Stand near his left shoulder (theoretically out of kicking range), take the lead line in your left hand (just under the clip), turn and raise the dressage whip toward his hip with your right hand. Hold the whip over his rear and further suggest forward motion by applying a light pressure to the lead rope with your left hand. Pause a beat with your arm outstretched, your body language suggesting "Walk forward." If you get no movement for a beat, kiss. If still nothing...

Tap your horse lightly, very lightly with the dressage whip on the rump. It's important to follow a rhythm, 1-2-3, 1-2-3, 1-2-3. It keeps you objective and following a protocol – as opposed to freaking out and smacking the devil out of them. It also teaches the horse that A is followed by B, B is followed by C: "If I ignore him when he kisses at me, he'll start up with that darn whip. I'll go ahead and move. Resistance is futile." If he's still parked out after ten or fifteen seconds, add a little more pressure with your tapping and pull his head slightly off to the side to offer and encourage sideways movement. Still nothing? Tap with a bit more intensity. I build up to "really irritating" (as opposed to painful, actual whipping) and stay with it till I get movement. (There are a few horses with the ability to get that back leg on their opposite side clear up to your chest at the speed of light. I've run across two such horses and this is why I max out my whip pressure at "irritating," staying well shy of an actual crack across the buttocks.) If one fly can drive your horse nuts with its incessant buzzing about, and a swarm of flies can cause a herd of buffalo to stampede, your colt will certainly know that you're asking for something here with your taps. You just have to be more stubborn than him.

The more adamant the horse is, the smaller "movement" you'll want to accept before dropping the whip and praising him. Look for small things, a lean, a dropping of the head, anything that suggests "forward" and build from there. Also, keep in mind the following advice from John Lyons: "First get the horse to move, then get it to move consistently, then get it to move consistently in the direction you want." What that means in this case is that any movement, sideways, backward, anything is good enough to get a release if your horse has been steadfastly refusing to budge. Once he learns that a raise of the whip means "move," (and that you're prepared to outlast him), it's not difficult to build on small improvements and to get onto the wash rack.

We'll desensitize the foal as we did before; we'll just substitute the feed bucket, hoof pick and hair brush for the hose, sponge and sweat scraper. You'll accustom him in one area of his body to the hose, for instance, then spread out from there, repeatedly returning to an area where he's comfortable with your touch, should he balk at some new approach, spot or object. Begin by rubbing his shoulders or withers with the end of the hose (turned off), working from there until he's comfortable with it moving around him. Mock the

actual motions you'll take later when scrubbing him
down. Don't forget to desensitize him to the feeling
of the hose moving around or reaching up and touching his back feet. (Any kicking back is a strong signal
that he's uncomfortable. Keep at your desensitizing
till there is absolutely no flinching.) Remember to
always begin your approach from a spot least likely to
startle him like his shoulders. Start at his shoulders,
then move up and over his back before running the
hose across his rump to his back legs, for instance.
Hoses have a strange, unpredictable way of moving,
with their coils and all, so they make great objects to
use for our practice.

When he's okay with the hose movement, turn it
on at a very light pressure. "Sack out" his shoulders,
withers, front legs and lower neck. If he balks as you
approach with the water streaming from the hose, hold
the hose as close as you can and take some water repeatedly into your palm. Rub the horse with that same
hand and he'll quickly allow the touch of the running
hose. If you get the hose over him and he feels the
water and he moves, do the best you can to keep the
water steadily streaming onto him. He shouldn't be
tied to anything so it's fairly simple to allow the horse
to move around you (even circling) while keeping the
hose on him. If you splash him with the hose and he
jumps and you remove the hose, what you've done is
said "Move and the water stops." Obviously we want
the opposite here, so if he moves hold the water on
him till he stands still.

Next, increase your pressure and work your way to
the rest of the foal. Start by aiming the hose along the
ground, bringing it to your horse's hoof, then away,
then farther up his leg, then away, etc. Advance, retreat,
advance, retreat. Or, crimp the hose in your hand,

killing most of the pressure; hold it to his shoulder and gradually unfold the hose. Think of this from his perspective: When he's hit by cold water, he's going to assume it's a forever thing and try to move away from it – just as when a saddle is first strapped to his back. You know it'll only last a moment – but he has no way of knowing that and will react accordingly, shying from the water or bucking the saddle. Help him understand that being hosed down is a temporary event by consciously and repeatedly advancing and retreating. More often than not, when they relax just long enough to actually "feel" the water, they'll realize it feels good and simply stand there. Note that, just like humans, horses can be rather sensitive about being hit with cold water in their, uh, nether-regions, so go easy there. When it comes time to soap the naughty bits, be ginger and keep an eye on your horse's attitude. (Cocked ears and rigid stances mean back off and go slower.) This is when you'll find out clearly whether you've spent enough time desensitizing between those back legs.

Okay, now the foal's head. Take a sponge, get it slightly wet and rub your horse's head with it. The dripping will cause some flinching, but work through it. Using a sponge to accustom him to water over his head is much easier than fighting with an unwieldy hose. You've only got water on the sponge (no soap), so you can rub around, under, and over the eyes, ears, and mouth. Remember when you first begin to start and stop, pause a beat; start and stop, pause a beat. Also, while you should make a special effort to work those ears back and forth, be careful not to cause water to drip unnecessarily down his ears. After all, they're really just great big holes on the top of his head; having water poured in there couldn't be all that pleasant. When you spritz the ears or head from some greater distance with the hose, he has the opportunity to fold his ears back and therefore protect himself; he's not afforded that protection with the sponge. I'll add yet another stutter step here when faced with an especially nervous horse by putting water first in my palm and rubbing the horse's head with my hand. He'll accept the sponge quickly then.

To get him used to water from the hose running over his head, turn the H_2O on just enough that it continues to lightly pour out even when held directly skyward. Hold the end of the running hose near the palm of your other hand and hold both up to your horse's head, repeatedly filling your palm and tipping it to allow the water to run down the horse's forehead and then from all around its head. Consciously cause more and more water (from your hand, from the hose, from the sponge) to flow over his eyes or down his head. Be careful not to shoot water directly up his nose or in such a way that you'll cause an undue amount to blast into his ear canal. (Adults may be remarkably good at pinning those ears back and closing off access – but we're dealing with a beginner here who has yet to learn all the tricks of self-preservation.) He may very well recoil when the running hose is first held over his muzzle. Deal with that by very, very quickly passing the hose over his head about one thousand billion times. He might throw his head up, but stick with it, spinning with him in the circles he'll no doubt turn. He'll soon realize he's overreacting and drop his head. (Remember, to desensitize, keep doing whatever you're doing until about 15 seconds after the horse shows signs of relaxing or stops moving his legs. Overt stiffness, showing the whites of its eyes, and a head held high are all telltale signs of a horse feeling some stress.)

Once your foal is calm and accepting of the simple shower concept, add soap to your bucket, grab up your sponge and get to work. Know that everything is new to him, so when trying something for the first time, (whether you're lathering the horse in thick shampoo bubbles, scraping sweat, or hosing it down) always start from a point that recent experience shows "He's okay with." You'll want to use a shampoo designed for human babies so as not to sting his eyes, make him sour on the whole experience and force you to rethink this whole "having horses" thing. Also, avoid over-soaping the underside (or inside) of his ears so as to avoid having to excessively rinse them later. When your colt is all sweet smelling, it's time to rinse him off and apply conditioner in the same way. (If you're following these directions with an older horse and you plan on riding him anytime soon, do yourself a favor and keep the conditioner away from the saddle area. Conditioner makes things slick and you'll likely spin right off your horse. Good for a laugh, sure, but dangerous.)

Finally, apply your sweat scraper. You might be tempted to figure "It's hot, I'll let him dry off naturally. He'll stay cooler longer." But, don't do it. A layer of water will trap heat and actually make the horse hotter. Need proof? When you get hot and start sweating, what do you normally do, over and over, almost subconsciously? You wipe the sweat off your forehead or the back of your neck. You're programmed to do that because it makes you cooler to remove that sweat. Same goes for your colt. Always scrape the water off on hot days.

End of Day Five

Section II: Additional Training

Further training for this stage of your horse's life

Teach Your Horse to Stand Tied

Follow this script – and in no time you'll be able to tie the horse that doesn't tie.

Note: Never tie a horse that hasn't been taught to stand tied calmly! (That includes trailer trips.) When you do tie your horse, always use a "quick-release" knot.

Whether you're training a baby that's a blank canvas or an old crank that's always pulled back, teaching your horse to stand tied calmly is simple and objective and just a matter of completing the steps I'll outline. Regardless of your horse's age, however, know going in that a mastery of **all material covered in the first four chapters, beginning with "Day One," is necessary**. Each one of those chapters represents a piece of the puzzle you're about to put together: You introduced your foal to the idea of giving to pressure and to reading your body language, you taught it to deal with scary objects when you sacked it out, and to deal with head shyness when you introduced the halter. Your youngster may not have a lot of training in it yet compared to it's older brothers or sisters – but if you've been following along and doing your homework, you two will sail through what follows.

Typically, when I'm asked how to train a horse to tie, I respond with "I don't specifically teach a horse to tie. I ride the horse and teach it to give better to the bit." Because when we ride, every single time we pick up those reins, we're conditioning the horse to either "give to pressure" or "not give to pressure" – and isn't that what tying is all about? If a horse can't be tied because it wants to pulls back – and that horse is currently being ridden – then I can virtually guarantee that it also pulls – hard – on those reins. It can't be tied, but it also can't be stopped or slowed when it doesn't want to be stopped or slowed. In such a case, you can teach the horse to tie – and improve your horse's performance in general – when you learn to make better use of your hands as you ride.

Of course, if you've got a baby that can't be ridden or an older horse that doesn't tie today but needs to stand tied in a trailer tomorrow, then there's a series of exercises to teach this specifically – and practicing them is time well-spent. Your horse's overall training will improve from a rider's viewpoint – but you'll also notice an improvement in ground manners as your horse begins to lead without dragging and lunge without stretching your arms. (And, by contrast, when you teach your horse to lunge or lead properly, you're also bettering its ability to stand tied.)

Before beginning, you should have the ability to cause your horse to stop and stand. Remember, as big and powerful as a horse is, there's no way on Earth for you to physically "make" the horse stand still. He's just too darn powerful (regardless his age), so you have to actively train it to do such a thing if you haven't already.

Considering all the work you've done by now, your colt is most likely looking for every opportunity to stand near you, hoping you won't put it to work. Still, you should test the control you have: Ask the horse to trot off and a beat or two later use your body language (or a very light bit of pressure on the longe line) to turn it back. Ask it to then keep two eyes on you as you walk around it in circles. If the horse easily passes such a test – if it turns back, stops, and follows you around on request – you should be good to move on. If not, ask it to do any ground work exercise you can think of. Keep its feet moving until it becomes the horse's idea to stop and stand. Be objective, don't just ask it to "move." Ask it to, let's say, take three steps back, two sideways, then one forward – and once you establish your pattern, do just exactly that, again and again and again. Or ask it to do repeated inside turns in the roundpen. Or to back away from you at an angle for the length of a football field. Practice anything, but do so in a business-like fashion; be kind and objective. When you do this, work at it in short segments of say 10 or 15 minutes, giving the horse a chance to stand quietly after each segment. If it moves off again, it's simply saying "I need more practice!" – so give it just that. If and when your horse is ready to stand, it's time to move on.

Step 1 builds on prior practice: Earlier, when you taught your horse to lead, you stood alongside it and simply applied a bit of pressure to the lead line until it looked toward you and relaxed its neck. Take that training a step further now by attaching a lunge line to your horse's halter, reeling out a good 10 or so feet of line, then sending the horse forward at a walk. Hold onto your end of the line, and when you feel the horse hit the end of it, ask it to turn back toward you, releasing your pressure entirely when you feel it relax through the neck. As the horse comes to the end of the slack, you want to slow it like a brake would slow a fine car – not suddenly with a jerk, but smoothly. Repeat that quick sequence until your youngster responds softly – and without hesitation – to the pressure you put on that line every time it's cued to move off. When you first begin this, you may find that the horse turns back toward you stiffly, it's body carried ramrod straight. With practice and in time, however, what you'll find is that the horse begins traveling in a relaxed frame, bending evenly throughout its entire body – like a giant snake or Stevie Wonder playing the piano. When you see that difference in the way your horse holds itself, that's your signal that your training is sinking in, taking hold – and things are improving. Practice this entire routine at a walk, then a trot and finally a lope.

(As you work on this, don't forget: The object here is to teach your horse to give to pressure. When it moves away from you, it is very important that you insist it keep going until it hits the end of the line and turns back in response to the several pounds of pressure you're applying. (You may need to energize it by asking for a bit more speed.) Repetition is equally important. Doing this many times will condition the horse to give to pressure automatically, without thinking about it.)

When you're ready, you need to solidify this "Turn and follow the pull you feel on the rope" business; you'll develop specific control over the hips and get a more relaxed horse as you do. (Never forget that the horse's power come from the drive of those hips; whether you're riding your horse or working it on the ground, they're often your key to control.) To do so, walk up close to a fence (stand back by about five feet), hold the lead in your left hand, a long dressage whip or carrot stick in your right, and ask the horse to travel counterclockwise at a walk between you and the fence. Ask it to travel to the left, swap the items in your hands, then ask it to travel back to the right.

Each time the horse passes you and hits the end of that line, ask it to **very specifically** turn those hips away, rotating over those front legs. You want to see the front of the horse remain relatively still as the back end swings around to affect the turn. If necessary, bring it's nose toward it's hip to give it the proper idea and tap it on the rear with your dressage whip if it fails to move around neatly. Keep practicing this – in both directions – until you find the right timing – and the horse understands fully that it must perform a smart turn on the forequarters. In a short while, what you'll find is that the horse begins to soften its neck; you won't even have to think about it. Relaxed neck muscles and a lower head carriage are natural bi-products of all your requests to swing those hips around.

Your horse will appear a bit timid when you first begin this simply due to the tight space you're asking it to work through. Your closeness to the wall or fence adds a bit of tension, asking the horse to overcome a natural bit of "claustrophobia." This is a good thing. Anything you can do here, under controlled circumstances, to exercise that "emotion muscle" in your horse's brain is going to pay dividends later. (This is a big reason why you're asked to practice many exercises at a trot and lope in addition to the walk. The faster speeds add excitement and amp the horse's emotions in a manner we control. As the excitement rises incrementally and his performance improves in kind, his ability to stay calm also grows incrementally. Doing something at a trot versus a walk might add an additional ten pounds of pressure – while a lope might add a hundred. Obviously, the horse that has learned to stay focused and in control through "100 pounds worth of pressure" is a better trained, safer horse to ride.)

Step 2: Your horse needs to learn to give to pressure in the direction from which it feels that pressure coming. It may be "used to" turning toward you because you're so often holding that lead line – but an older horse can step on dropped reins and maybe you'd like to place your youngster in the cross-ties. Horses have got to learn to give and turn toward the source of the pull when it's not you. To do that, move back at a 45 degree angle to the horse instead of directly to the side as before (you'll be standing away facing its hindquarters now) and put pressure on the line until the horse turns, softens, and faces you. (If the horse wants to turn toward you before you can take your position, simply hold your hand up as if to say "halt" and pressure it to move back and stand correctly with your body positioning as you practiced back in "Day One.") Practice asking the horse to turn and face you from that 45 degree angle a few times then step directly behind the horse and do the same.

Keep moving around the horse, circling. Reposition yourself and pause every few feet or so to apply pressure and ask it to turn toward you – and keep doing so until the rope or line is actually wrapped completely around the horse by one full revolution. When you've worked your way all the way around – and the horse has obviously learned to follow the pressure on the line regardless of where you're standing at the moment you apply your pressure – run through all these steps again. This time, however, with each position you take (as you work your way around), reel out ten or so feet of line as necessary, then ask the horse to move off before hitting the end of the line and turning back. Ask it to do this first at a walk, then trot, then lope.

Step 3: Wrap your lunge line around a sturdy post. When you do this, give it just one easy "wrap" around; don't bring the rope around multiple times yet. The horse should be able to easily pull back if it panics. You're about to do both of the first two steps again, but now the line flows from your hands, around the post, then to the horse.

With the line wrapped and the horse simply standing there, move back and apply pressure to the line, releasing it when the horse turns its head toward the post and you feel it soften through its neck. Keep repeating this and, every few moments, reposition the horse in such a way that you practice asking it to give and soften at increasingly sharp angles – just as you did earlier when you held the line directly.

After a few minutes, begin asking the horse to move off: Standing on the horse's left, send it off to the right, at progressively higher speeds, asking it to turn back toward the pressure it feels. Note that you don't want to hold so tightly to the line that the horse hits the end of it and gets jerked back abruptly as if hitting a wall. Instead, each time, slowly take hold, just as a brake slowly slows and then finally stops your car. When you can stand to the left of your horse and send it off to the right – and it dutifully and softly turns back to you at varying speeds, flip the rope over the horse's body and send it off again; this time you're on the left and the horse moves to the left.

Next, send the horse away and ask it to turn back, but when it turns back this time, apply light pressure and encourage it to take a step toward the post, dropping your pressure when the horse moves (or thinks of moving) a single step forward. With a bit less space now between it and the post, ask it to again move off and turn back. Keep repeating this – and do so from both sides of the horse – asking it to step in closer and closer, moving off and turning back, until it's standing with but a foot of rope between its nose and the post.

Finally, understand that you can't really say that your horse "ties" when the only proof you have is that it stands "tied" (quote/unquote) under ideal conditions. It's the unexpected tipped over garbage can or wound-up dog that we need to build protection against. To finish your training then, actively work to desensitize the horse as it stands with the line wrapped around a post, (not tied) to things or events that might cause it to become startled and pull back under typical-for-you conditions. Ask yourself, what might come into con-tact with your horse – purposely or by accident – that might frighten it? Who or what might walk, run, or stumble by that might cause a fright? Assemble as many of these things as you can (or reasonable facsimiles of these things) – and get your horse "used to" giving to the pressure he feels coming from that tied line despite this additional excitement. Remember that if you take away a stimulus while the horse's feet are mov-ing, you've actually sensitized it to that thing. You've taught it to move or run away from that particular object or happening. By contrast, if you take away that same stimulus only after the horse has stopped moving his feet (and ideally kept that stimulus up for another 15 or so seconds), then you've desensitized – or "dulled" – the horse.

To do this, assemble 20 or 30 "scary things," ranging from barely scary like your curry comb – to real scary like a popping balloon or a sack tied to the end of your carrot stick (that gets whipped about). Position your horse near your post, your line wrapped around the post, the end of it in your hand. (**Warning! Under**

no circumstances should you or a friend ever hold the line from outside the pen! Were you to become entangled in that rope as the horse panics and pulls back, you would have a serious problem.) Take up your items, one at a time, and desensitize your horse to each by rubbing them against your horse, waving them about, dropping them at its feet, pitching them side to side, and smacking them against each other. Do anything you can think of no matter how strange it might seem to your neighbors. See if you can't get a bit of a rise in those emotions, but not so much that his feet move, then bring the object away. Purposely raise and lower those emotions. Raise and lower them as if strengthening a muscle through exercise. Any time the horse pulls back, keep rubbing or waving the object you're currently holding and cling to the lunge line the best you reasonably can; release it only when the horse turns back toward the source of the pressure and relaxes. If you have to let go for safety's sake, simply reposition yourselves and start over. When you can see that your horse has come to respect – and without hesitation gives to – the pull it feels, you're ready to tie for real.

Horses that Bite

Biting is the worst vice a horse (of any age) can have. Here's what to do about it.

Biting is more dangerous than bucking, than rearing, than kicking – more dangerous than anything else you can name. A horse can nip off a finger, an ear, or objects I can't mention in mixed company in half an instant. It can do so without warning and lightning fast. Greased lightning fast. Never forget: It's a prey animal with the reflexes of a prey animal.

Prevention is your first line of defense when it comes to biting. Know that your horse would never, ever bite its own mother and see this as an issue of a horse that does not respect its human. Turn that dynamic around by setting up a zero-tolerance policy. Watch for moments when you are being disrespected and deal with infractions immediately. When you walk from A to B and your horse blocks your path, it gets out of your way, not the other way around. When you feed, you don't ignore the actions of a horse that rushes up rudely, bullying you with its shoulders. Instead, you set it back – literally and figuratively – with the dressage whip you carry for just such occasions. When it pins its ears as you buckle the halter, put that horse to work at once and do so intensely: Do any ground work exercise you know, for ten or so minutes, and show it that tranquility can only be had when deference is shown. A good thing to do any time your horse crosses the line is to simply back it up. Back it for a football field or two and remind it clearly that you pay the bills.

If your horse has begun biting, or it's "mouthy" and you fear it might morph into something more aggressive, then do each of the following to protect yourself:

1) Until and unless your horse becomes a model citizen, allow it no time to stand around looking for problems to cause. When it's with you, find it a job and keep it busy. Practice any ground maneuvers you'd like to make better. Ask it to move its shoulders, to back, to disengage its hind end... anything, just keep it busy.

2) This goes without saying, but a reminder couldn't hurt: Keep your horse's teeth consciously positioned away from you when it's in your presence. The easiest and most objective way to do this is to insist that it stay a few feet away from you at all times. Have your safe zone and insist that it maintain a distance.

3) Any time the horse gets mouthy – in fact, any-time you even think it's thinking about it – recall the cartoon skunk that fell in love with the black cat. She couldn't stand him. He'd hug her tightly, oblivious to her wriggling frantically to get away. He was in love; she thought he stunk. Literally.

To proactively fix your biting problem, you'll be the skunk and your horse the cat. Start looking for excuses and the next time it signals its displeasure at anything for half an instant, drop what you're doing, reach for its nose and rub that snout between your palms like you're trying to start a fire. Pet and rub and massage like you're trying to scrub the chrome off a trailer hitch. Pet until it takes its head away – and then grab it back and do it some more.

Push your horse a little. Dare it to show aggravation – and the moment it does, give it all the attention it seems to be looking for and more; pet it feverishly and until it screams "enough!" and tries to pull away. Have fun with this and look for every opportunity to do it. Doing so makes you "active." No longer are you waiting for an attack. Now you're in the driver's seat – now you get respect.

Tip: This same "fix" works with horses that act like jerks when cinched up. The next time you pull the cinch tight and the horse responds by throwing its head up, dancing around or gnashing its teeth, try taking its muzzle in your hands and rubbing it incessantly. (Note however, that if your horse reacts negatively to the sight of your saddle, first make sure that the saddle fits correctly and not causing pain. Don't expect it to "get over" a painful fit.)

The beauty of this method is this: First, acting like the teasing older sister or brother, antagonizing your horse, is just plain fun. Second, you'll see that the horse you once feared anytime it nosed around, now minds its own business, hoping you don't notice it and start getting all weird again.

Picking Up Feet

Teaching your horse to lift its feet on cue is really very simple. Here's how.

Training a horse to pick up its feet is super-easy when we set ourselves up for success. Yet battles over such a thing play out in barn aisles everywhere all the time: "Why can't this dumb horse just pick up its feet and stand still?!" It seems so simple to us humans... until we look at it from their prey animal point of view: Allowing a predator (that'd be you) to grab a foot means he can't run away and that could mean a grisly death. You'd be nervous too, had you been somebody else's dinner since the dawn of time. Consequently, empathy is the name of the game here. You've got thirty years ahead of you with your horse, so be accepting and patient now as you spend a day or two working to gain his trust.

Before tackling today's topic, make absolutely sure that your horse has been thoroughly sacked out to your touch. If that little voice in your head says there is any way your horse is going to react negatively to your touch (if it might flinch, freeze up, pull away, try to kick, etc.) especially when working around those back feet, then... you ain't ready. Conversely, if you're hearing "All systems go," then you should have an easy time of it.

You can teach the following very simply without a round pen – but the round pen offers two significant advantages: 1) You don't have to juggle a lead line in one hand, and 2) Should the horse need a little extra motivation to play along, you can more easily send him around a few rotations.

Let's begin with the back feet. We'll set the stage for success by first working to get the horse relaxed and keeping weight off our target foot: Standing on the horse's left side and holding the lead, ask it to move its hips away, pivoting over its shoulders. (Apply pressure to the lead line, bringing the horse's nose toward its hips if need be to cause it to step around.) Ask him to take a step or two and when he stops, look at the back leg closest to you (the one you'd like to pick up). Does he have any weight on it? Keep asking him to move and then pausing until, by chance, he stands with that nearest back leg cocked up. You've seen this stance a million times, a horse standing on three feet, the fourth resting, slightly turned up, toe on the ground, heel in the air.

If he comes to a flat-footed stop, get him moving again immediately, but don't be in a hurry. You should be ultra-relaxed as you do this, almost comically so; your motions, the horse's motions should look to the casual observer like he or she is watching a film in "slow motion." You also wanna be extra-patient: This initial step might take 10, 20, 30 or even more attempts before the horse happens upon the correct answer the first time. (And you may very well think it impossible in the interim.) But, once he figures out the pattern and what you're after, he'll begin consistently shifting the weight off the leg at your request. In fact, in just a short time, you'll find that merely asking the horse to bring its head an inch or two toward its hips will cue it to cock that leg.

Each time the horse stops correctly, release any pressure on the lead line and begin petting the horse's withers. As you do, keep an eye on that back leg and, as long as it stays cocked, keep petting. Work your way along the horse's back, over it's rump, and down toward the back leg. Using two hands then, rub the hock and cannon areas of the back leg nearest you vigorously as if trying to warm or massage the leg. (Keep your head tipped away from those kicking legs as common sense dictates.) After a moment or two, rub your way back up to your starting point (the horse's withers) before pausing and repeating just this sequence. Spend at least ten minutes doing nothing but this, petting the horse from it's withers down it's back and rump, rubbing a back leg between your hands, then petting your way back to the withers. The horse **must** keep that back leg cocked the entire time you do this. If and when it goes flat-footed, immediately stop what you're doing, reposition the horse correctly, and start over.

Next, start rubbing again at the withers and work your way back – but this time, when you have "petted your way" around and down to the hind leg, lightly grasp the fetlock or heel portion of the hoof itself and see if you can't "suggest" that it lift the foot off the ground an inch or two. If the horse has that leg cocked, no weight will be on the foot and so picking it up here is a simple thing to do. After a very brief moment, let it drop on its own and pat your way back to the head. Repeat this process, gradually asking for more, moving and repositioning the horse anytime he goes "flatfooted" on you. With each repetition, try your best to release the foot one beat before you think he's about to pull it away, showing him that handing over his foot is not a forever thing.

When you let go of the horse's foot, you should do just that: Let go. If the foot drops a time or two, he'll quickly learn to hold it himself, rather than developing the annoying habit of placing more and more weight on you as a crutch. Being overly concerned about our horse's balance is a major cause of leaning. Trust me, he doesn't want to tip over and is more than capable of standing squarely, so to speak, on three feet. If the horse knows that you can and will drop his foot at any time, he'll learn not to lean.

To train the front feet, stand at the horse's left shoulder, hold the lead line or rein about six inches under the horse's mouth and raise a dressage whip up over its hip. Kiss and begin tapping lightly, but grow your taps progressively harder until the horse walks forward. After a few beats, use the grip in your left hand to bring the horse's chin toward the point of its shoulder and to then ask it to step its shoulders away from you. If you just can't get those shoulders moving off, you can alternatively ask the horse to simply back up   though this will make the next step in the process a bit more challenging.

In either case, use common sense, timing, and luck to ask the horse to stop moving, leaving little-to-no weight on the front left leg as it does. Do not look for it to stop and stand with its front leg cocked   but do look for it to keep the weight off that leg. If possible then, run your hand down the back of its leg and bring the leg up and forward by cupping your hand behind it's knee and pulling. If the horse has shifted its weight back onto that leg, ask it to move about again. In time, your horse will realize that standing, allowing its leg to be handled, is easier than doing your strange little dance. Stick with it and keep asking for that hoof until the horse learns the pattern. Given enough practice, you'll find yourself cueing it to actually lift its own foot by simply leaning over and touching its leg.

When the horse will obligingly pick up it's four feet to have them each picked clean, it's time to prepare for the first professional trim. Farriers hold feet for longer periods of time than we riders do, they bend legs into more exaggerated positions – they make more noise than fifty garbage cans tumbling down a metal staircase. They also have schedules to keep and no time to train your horse for you, (not that you should you expect him or her to anyway), so it's a good thing to do just a bit more training: Start simply by holding the foot up for increasingly longer periods of time, at "odder angles," and tapping the hoof and soul with your hoof pick or just a rock you pick up. Mock the classic shoer stance by bringing the leg up and laterally away from the horse's body, placing it between your own legs as the farrier does and tap the hoof some more. Keep the hoof raised and **carefully** desensitize the horse to the strange sounds it might hear: Drag a feed bucket back and forth across the floor, bang metal against metal, maybe throw in a sporadic "Aagh, my aching back" if you're looking for true realism. The work you do to prepare for the first farrier visit won't take but a handful of minutes – and it's the polite thing to do.

Finally, let's teach your horse to lift any of its legs when you simply point. Teaching your horse to pick up its feet by remote control is more than a neat trick. If you've spent any time at all under a horse, you know how quickly they learn to lean on us and take advantage: We lift the leg, holding it up using 2, 5, or 10 pounds of support and it quickly learns to lean with 3, 6 or 11 pounds. This is us "expecting less and getting less." Instead, let's ask the horse to raise its own leg. Let's start "expecting more."

Start at your horse's front left shoulder where there's less chance you might be kicked: Take a dressage whip, point to its front left leg, kiss (the kiss says "move something"), and tap the leg exactly five times with super-light pressure. Stop immediately if the horse shifts its weight even coincidentally; that's all you're looking for at this point. But when or if it doesn't, tap a little bit firmer another five times at the same pace. Repeat this sequence, tapping and incrementally adding more pressure until the horse shifts its weight. There's not a whole lot of "meat" on a horse's leg so I'll tap varying parts of its leg, spending most of the time tapping the upper, more muscled area   especially if I have to use a little more force.

It is absolutely imperative that you follow a pattern: Tap five times lightly, tap harder five times, tap still harder five times and so forth with all your tapping done at exactly the same pace. Don't ever say to yourself "Charger's not gonna do it" and simply smack the horse right off the bat. Doing so will cause your horse to lose respect for you. Giving it every opportunity to do as you ask by building your pressure **slowly** builds respect. Remember this advice when you run low on patience.

At first, accept a weight shift; minutes later you should be looking for the hoof to actually lift. Each time the horse advances, ask for a bit more "of a lift." If it stalls out at a certain height, don't stop your tapping, keep at it until the leg moves higher.

You might try taking your lead rope and wrapping it very loosely (so that it would drop off should the horse walk off) around the bottom of its leg. Apply a little pressure to this rope, suggesting that it lift its leg as you kiss, then tap. This often helps speed up the process.

When the horse consistently lifts its foot to the tap, drop the whip, but hold out your arm as if still carrying it. Kiss and move your arm as if tapping. Of course, the first few times you'll need to revert to using the whip to back up your request   but that's where a light tug on the rope can help out. Be careful to look for very slight improvement at first; maybe it just shifts its weight or bends at the knee. Reward every little improvement and your horse will soon be lifting its leg following a kiss and a point.

You'll use the same system to work your way around the horse, teaching the concept to all four feet. (Be sure to stand near a shoulder where there's less chance of being kicked   even when you're working on those back legs.) Note that if you start with the front left foot, then move to another, you might be surprised to find that your kiss and point don't mean "lift the leg I point at." Instead, it'll mean (to your horse) "lift the front left foot." You'll need to train each leg individually.

This can all get pretty funny as you work your way around. Your horse will typically resort to doing what got it a release the last time you made a similar request. So, when you first begin with the fourth leg, it might very well lift all of the other three before that fourth leg. It'll look like it's dancing and the fact is, if you want to take this a step further and teach your horse "to dance," this is exactly how you'd do it; you'd point to one then the other in quick succession.

When your horse understands "Lift that leg when I point to it," begin moving away at a 45 degree angle to the horse's body. Kiss and point at a two foot distance, then three and so on. Before long you'll be able to stand thirty feet away, "at your horse's four corners," and cause it to lift any leg on command. Your farrier will love it.

Sidepassing to You On the Ground

This trick, with its huge "wow" factor, is actually easy to teach to any horse – young or old! (And it's a great fix for horses that won't stand still at the mounting block!)

Have you ever seen a horse that's been trained to actually sidepass **toward** the trainer? The trainer stands there next to her horse   and as she backs away from it, the horse sidesteps its entire body toward her. It's easily one of the coolest tricks I've ever seen, like something that took years of training and maybe a little black magic. The funny thing is though, this trick is actually one of the simpler things to teach. If your horse has good ground manners and will currently backup and move its shoulders away from you on command, you can easily train it to "side pass toward you" in just a few sessions of about one hour each.

Note: This exercise involves steps that can cause the ill-mannered horse to challenge you. If your horse isn't easily managed on the ground, if its shoulders can't be moved away and it can't be backed up lightly, then shelve this exercise until you've done more ground work. Horses that lead well and horses that load on and off trailers smoothly are good candidates. A bad candidate is a horse that drags you around or plows you aside with its shoulders. If your horse thinks it's the boss of you, don't even try this. Spend the time it takes to teach basic control on the ground. Get that solid, then return to this more advanced material. When you're able to walk your horse past a group of beckoning buddies or honking cars or barking dogs without your pulse quickening, you should be ready.

You'll want to use a snaffle bit and reins as opposed to simply using a halter and lead line. We'll be motivating our horse to move its legs, then attempting to channel the direction in which it moves. The bit will offer a clearer signal than a halter should the horse become confused and a tad agitated. You'll also need the aid of a dressage whip and a good solid wall or fence. Nice flat, high walls, the type you find in the typical riding arena, are the best.

Throughout this entire chapter, you will be on the left side of the horse, the wall will be on the right side of the horse. Our initial goal will be to cause the horse to swing its hips away from the wall. Simply reverse everything later to "educate" its right side. If you pause for a moment now and picture that   your horse alongside a wall, swinging its hips away from that wall   the rest of this material will be easy.

Begin by positioning your horse parallel to and about one foot away from the wall, and take the rein in your left hand about 6-8 inches from the horse's mouth. Kiss and raise the dressage whip in your right hand up above your horse's left hip as if a conductor without an orchestra. Begin walking backwards, in effect leading your horse. As you move, keep a watchful eye on its back left hoof   the one nearest you   and think "Step over and to your left." Your horse will continue walking forward, oblivious, thinking something akin to "I'm starved" or "Gotta poop." After a beat, begin tapping super lightly on its hip.

Keep moving and staring at that hoof. Use your grip on the rein and do not allow the horse to get any closer to your body than it is at this very moment   not at any point in this training. When or if it ignores your request to step to its left (after, say, 20 seconds), tap with a bit more intensity.

Consistency is everything here. You must develop a pattern and a rhythm to that pattern: If you begin by raising your hand, pausing, kissing, and tapping, then ten minutes later you should still be following that exact flow and pattern. The horse will quickly learn that "tapping" always follows "kissing" and a pause always follows the raising of your arm. Rather than wait around to get tapped, it'll start moving off as you raise your arm.

Right about now you're wondering "How the heck does Flicka know which direction to move her feet?" It's simple: When we turn up the pressure with our taps   but don't allow the horse to move forward any faster   that energy's gotta go somewhere and your friend Flicka has only got six directions to choose from: Up, down, backwards, forwards, left and right. You're keeping her forward movement in check with the position of your body and hold on the rein; the wall blocks her to the right and, of course, "up" and "down" are not true options. That leaves "left" as the only choice.

Until you get the step you're looking for, you'll continue upping your pressure every twenty or thirty seconds till the horse moves its back leg correctly. You're not hitting it then or at any time   you're "annoying" it with your taps in the same way that a fly on its lip might. When or if we're ignored, we simply progressively "add more flies." We tap quicker with a bit more intensity, we kiss louder, and so on, until the horse complies. If a sister can drive her brother nuts simply by staring at him, you can certainly motivate a horse to take a step with a dressage whip in your hand.

You'll continue walking backwards, tapping your horse till it moves its foot one single step to the left however small that step might be   then releasing and repeating. Learning to take that very first sideways step is the hardest part for the horse, so be extra patient when you begin. Be quick on your release and reward it for even the tiniest improvements. Once it gets the idea, things go quickly.

At first, the horse will take a step to the left then immediately move back against the wall. But in time, after you've asked it repeatedly in quick succession to swing its hips out, it'll realize it's easier to travel at an angle to the wall, sidepassing to its left.

Remember, it's your quick release that both rewards the horse and tells it "That's what I'm looking for, right there." It's paramount that you release your pressure as quickly as possible and that you both relax for several seconds while you pet and praise. If you fail to take breaks and just keep marching around the arena, the horse will simply tune you out.

If you're going around and around and the horse doesn't seem to be improving, then one of two things is happening: Either you're not applying enough pressure or the horse is in fact improving and you're looking for too much too fast. Practice a bit longer and watch the horse carefully. Remember, you're only looking for tiny, tiny, tiny improvements in the beginning. The horse might step just a hair in the right direction and it might do so for just a fraction of a second, literally.

If that's the case, all you've got to do is learn to accept less at this early stage. Stop tapping and praise the very instant **you even think** you've seen a correct step and you'll begin seeing rapid improvement in no time.

On the other hand, if the horse isn't trying, if it's simply walking forward dead-headed, then that's another matter entirely. Simply put, your horse isn't motivated. Add more intensity to those taps. Most likely you're being too timid. Being too timid is nagging and horses lose respect for you quickly when you nag. You'll still want to start with very light taps, but build to a higher intensity than applied previously. You've got to wake the horse up; let it know you mean business. (But be careful and watch your positioning when you apply your "extra pressure" so as not to get kicked.)

Be aware of the pressure your horse is putting on your left hand. If you feel as if you're being pushed out of the way, stop what you're doing and spend time reinforcing good ground manners: Step into the center of the arena and tap the horse on its hip, asking it to step forward. Allow it to take several steps before asking it to turn its hips away by bringing its nose toward its hip. After the horse swings around, but before all the energy leaves its body, ask it to step off in another direction. For example, you might ask it to swing its hips away, then take several steps sideways (away from you), then backward and finally forward before releasing your grip. Be creative and practice just this for twenty minutes, mixing up the directions you ask for. Be sure to reward your horse through a lessening of rein pressure anytime you feel the neck soften or the feet move lightly. Don't be afraid to use progressively harder tapping to add necessary motivation. Repeat this until you feel the horse begin to move in each direction as if sliding on ice   then head back to your wall.

When you can back away from your horse and it'll consistently sidestep toward you, keeping its hips ninety degrees from the wall, you're ready for the next step: Move five feet away from the wall and repeat the entire process in exactly the same way. (Don't be tempted to move too far away   you still need that wall to make corrections.)

The moment you move off the wall your training will unravel. You'll tap   and the horse will probably swing in the wrong direction entirely, away from the tapping and to its right because the wall's not there to block it. This is to be expected. When this happens, simply keep your pressure up, smoothly directing the horse through your grip on the rein back toward the wall, tapping until it correctly steps its hip to its left. Pet and praise and move away from the wall before trying again, repeating this process until your horse understands what you're after.

From here it's a simple matter to move away from the wall entirely. Walk to the center of the arena and repeat the entire training process. Your horse may again regress a bit, but all you have to do is "go back to the wall" (either against it as when you first began, or away by several feet) till things start to click. Put an increasing amount of space between you and the horse and eventually it'll be working off your gestures alone.

Finally, you may be wondering… From this point forward, how will my horse know when to move toward me and when to move away? The answer simply lies in the horse reading your body language. You will have practiced this enough that your equine friend will have little trouble knowing exactly what you're looking for.

Teach Your Horse to Come to You

Rather than chasing your horse around the pasture, wouldn't it be a lot easier to whistle and let it come to you?

Note: The directions which follow describe work in the round pen. Know that you can do everything I'm about to describe without a round pen by attaching the horse to a longe line and adapting as necessary. Note also that this material can be done with a horse of any age – but if you're training a weanling, all work should be done at a walk or trot. (Remember our rule when working a young foal: If you see it sweat, you're working it too hard.)

Throw a rope across your horse at its withers. If you look down, you'll see that you're either on one side of that rope or the other. Lock that image in your brain because your body positioning is everything as we move ahead in our training: If you walk toward your horse from one side of the rope you'll push the hips away or the entire horse forward. If you approach the horse from the other side of the rope, your body language will slow the horse's forward movement or you'll push the front half of the horse away. Likewise, retreating from the shoulder from the same side of the rope will help "draw" the front of the horse towards you. To do your training, you'll have to consciously be on one side of that line or the other – which side simply depends on the task at hand.

Begin by asking for an inside turn: Get the horse circling (let's say to the left, so counterclockwise) at a fast trot, (or preferably at a walk if working with a weanling). As the horse comes around, lift your "outside" arm as if to peel it away from the fence and toward the center of the ring. If it correctly turns in, motion for it to keep going around in the new direction. Practice this, getting your "inside turns," until your horse easily reads your body language and turns in when lightly prompted. If you're using a longe line (as opposed to running the horse loose in a round pen), teach it to turn based on your body language – not by pulling on the line.

If your horse moves haltingly, dawdles, or stops entirely, do what it takes to keep it moving at the quicker pace you initially established. If it incorrectly makes an "outside turn" – which is, to say, it turns away from you or toward the fence, quickly move to your right, and ask the horse to turn back to the proper direction. Let it go one half-turn around the pen before asking again. This will give you a moment to collect your thoughts and, perhaps more importantly, keep you from just running about like the proverbial headless chicken. It'll keep you proactive rather than reactive.

Inside turns can be tough to get consistently so here are three tips: First, be mindful of your body language. Keep your hips parallel to the motion of the horse and be careful to not walk directly at its neck when you want it to turn inside. (You walk directly at the head or neck only when you want an **outside** turn.) Second, be lightening-fast with your corrections. If you ask for "inside" and the horse turns "outside," jump like a scalded cat to get it going back the correct way. Third, pay attention to how fast you "back off" when your horse does something correct. Anytime it completes the inside turn properly, for example, release your pressure instantly.

As you progress, begin picking random spots on the fence and ask your horse to turn exactly at that spot. When you can cause it to turn at each small spot you choose, pick two spots on either side of the pen and ask the horse to turn after rounding half the pen. The two of you should drill as a team until you're the very picture of precision. Gradually bring your two spots closer together until the turn itself is removed and the horse stays looking at you as it jukes to and fro like a football player.

At that point, you'll find that there is a moment when the horse hesitates, in effect wondering if it should turn away or not. By now, it would love to stop and take a breather – so take advantage of that momentary pause and, in that instant, back away from the horse, suggesting that it stop with your body language. After it stops, ease back up to it and pet it. Let it know that stopping and standing is okay – and, in fact, exactly what you wanted.

With the horse stopped and facing you, your goal becomes simply this: Get it to look at you with two eyes. Keeping two eyes on you means the horse is tuned into you – not the exit, not the filly in the next pen. You must insist on "two eyes" throughout this next part whenever you make a request.

Stand in front of your horse and ask it to look at you with both eyes. If it's looking away, get its attention by calling out, waving your arms, snapping your fingers... whatever you have to do. Pause and wait. In a moment or two it will make the "mistake" of looking away – which is a good thing because mistakes are just opportunities to teach. The moment it looks off, call the two eyes back again. If your horse is prone to running around like a spaz case, then take it easy and use what little it takes to get the eyes back on you. But, by the same token, don't be afraid to be as assertive as necessary, even if it means sending it back around the pen for several revolutions. It is vital that your horse not be allowed to ignore you.

We want the horse to follow us with those two eyes no matter where we go, so next you'll take a step to its left or right. If you move and the horse looks away, bring its gaze back to you. Keep inching further to the side, bringing those two eyes with you, eventually causing the horse to turn its entire body to face you. It won't take long before it begins following your movements about the pen. As it gets the hang of it, try moving quicker, walking circles around the horse. This has the effect of solidifying the concept of "Look at me no matter where I go" in the horse's mind.

By now, you should have noticed a pretty cool by-product of all this work: When the horse turns to you, it no longer turns its body stiffly, but rather its neck muscles have softened and there's a bend throughout the entire body, like a snake rounding a tree. The odds are excellent that it's also creeping in toward you. These are excellent signs that you're earning the horse's respect – and that you're ready for the next step.

Ask the horse to keep two eyes on you as you walk toward its hips. It will pivot over its front end and, as the two of you move, keep your own two eyes on the horse's hind legs. When the leg closest to you crosses in front of the other, turn away and walk off. Pause. Pet. Repeat: Ask the hips to move away and keep them moving until the back leg **closest to you crosses in front of the other**. When the horse will consistently place the leg closest to you in front of the other **three** steps in a row, you're ready to move on – but don't push too hard, too fast. Don't ask for two steps until you can get just one every time you ask; don't ask for three until you get two.

As you practiced your inside turns, did you notice how your horse began to cut corners, running in through the center, each time coming closer to you? As long as your horse isn't being aggressive, that's actually a good thing – and we'll use it now to our advantage:

Send the horse out on a circle, lets say to the left. As it comes around, ask it to turn in toward you as if an inside turn – but ask it to stop, facing you. When you step in front of the horse the first few times, it might pull up and stop rather abruptly, near the wall – and at quite some distance from where you stand. To encourage it to come nearer, start asking it to move faster around the circle and adjust your own positioning in such a way that the horse is given little choice but to head straight at you. (Needless to say, you'll need to factor in plenty of common sense here for safety's sake.) Repeat this entire sequence until the horse peels off the wall, off its path, and comes directly toward you. Each time the horse comes to a stop, ease over to it, pet it and allow it to stand and relax for a full minute.

If the horse veers away from you as it turns in, allow it to go around and try again. If it wanders away from you as the two of you are standing taking a break, send it circling again and really make it hustle. Send the same wake-up call anytime the horse seems to quit trying or otherwise sleepwalk through your practice. Consciously, proactively, make it clear to the horse: "Stand near me and rest – or run fast circles over there."

A quick note about petting your horse in the round pen: Don't approach it like some sneaky cartoon character, creeping up slowly, with lots of "there theres." Your creepy movements signal to the horse – a prey animal – that something's amiss and it won't trust you. Instead, just walk up and pet it; don't make a big deal out of it. If it runs away, remind yourself that you're in a pen that's round. It can run, but where's it gonna go?

When you see that the horse is no longer simply running around the perimeter of the pen, but is in fact looking to turn in toward you, change things up a bit. Instead of going over to the horse each time it stops, begin actively encouraging it to close up that distance itself by coming **to you**. Wait till it comes to a stop on its own, then encourage it to come the rest of the way to you by kissing and snapping your longe whip if it doesn't move some body part. (Remember, your kiss doesn't mean "Come to me," it means "Move something." Practice, context and your body language tell the horse "which something" to move.) The horse might move toward you – or away from you. If it moves away, bring it back by requesting an inside turn. Otherwise, keep motivating it to move – and to move toward you.

At some point, you'll find that, despite your efforts, the horse just stops getting any closer like there's an invisible barrier between you. When this happens, break the stalemate by using what you practiced earlier: Walk towards its hip and ask that hip to move away, the back leg nearest you crossing in front of the other. Get several side steps, then go to the opposite side of the horse and do the same thing. You may need to go back and forth, from one side to the other, quite a few times. Doing this actually forces the horse to creep forward to within easy touching distance just as a corkscrew removes a cork from a bottle turn by turn.

Practice asking the horse to travel around the pen and turn in toward you, breaking any stalemates with the "move the hips" trick discussed – until it very clearly understands that you'd like it to come directly up to you. It's actually quite easy: Always speak kindly and never purposely scare the horse – but be firm in your corrections. Otherwise, follow the directions as outlined; there are basically just two components: Keep your pressure up – and make it very clear that it can relax only near you.

When the horse will come to you following a spin around the round pen, teach it to come to you from a standstill: Ask it to stand perpendicular to the wall of the pen, facing in toward the center. If need be, use a series of inside turns to stop it in that position, then turn and walk to the center of the pen. If it follows you, and it very likely will, then "shoosh" it back into position, holding up your hand as if to say "halt" until it stays put. You may need to be aggressive (asking for rapid fire turns until it gets the idea), but it's important that the horse learns to approach you only when invited.

Stand in the center of the round pen and kiss to the horse. If it simply stares at you, then get its hips moving (one side, then the other, as earlier) to convey the idea that we want it to move forward. You might also try sending it around the pen, then immediately asking for an inside turn, suggesting with your body language that it come to you, just as you previously practiced. Be determined, and the horse will now quickly begin to associate your kiss with "come to me" due to all the work done earlier. To finish, gradually increase the distance from which you make your request.

To add icing on the cake, teach the horse to trot or even lope to you from a standing start. Doing so is simply a matter of teaching a bit of speed control and then charging the horse with energy:

First, practice asking the horse to travel half-trips around the pen at alternating speeds. Pick some random speed within your chosen gait (be that a trot or lope) and turn the horse after half a trip around the pen, asking it to travel at a totally different, random speed still within your chosen gait. Be sure to kiss each time you ask for faster – and if you want to slow it, do so by asking for a turn. You do not want it to travel so far that it slows on its own, but if it does, speed it up a few beats, then ask it to turn and move off at another random speed. Spend the time it takes to teach the horse that each time you kiss, it must move faster – and "faster" **must mean** a "noticeable change of leg speed." If you don't actually see the horse move faster one beat after asked, be quick with a snap of the whip.

Next, pack energy into the horse by sending it out and around the pen at a faster rate than you'll be looking for later when it's asked to come to you. (Because the stored energy's going to dissipate.) Keep your actions friendly but really make it hustle and it'll carry through at speed when it turns in to come to you. Pause only briefly in order to keep the horse charged up, then ask several more times in quick succession. Kiss to it any time you need more speed and always back up your kiss with motivation when necessary. Finally, stop it on one side of the pen, go to the other side and energetically give it your cue to "come." If the horse moves toward you too slowly, speed it up with a kiss – or by sending it around the pen at a much faster clip, then stop it for just a short moment and ask again. Remember, the energy you put in is the energy you get out.

Books by This Author

Check out these titles from Keith Hosman

- Crow Hopper's Big Guide to Buck Stopping
- Get On Your Horse: Curing Mounting Problems
- Horse Tricks
- How to Start a Horse: Bridling to 1st Ride
- Round Penning: First Steps to Starting a Horse
- Trailer Training
- What I'd Teach Your Horse (Basic Training)
- What Is Wrong with My Horse? (Problem Solving)
- When Your Horse Rears... How to Stop It
- Your Foal: Essential Training

Available in all major formats, including:

Paperback | Kindle | Nook | Kobo | Apple | Audio

Purchase 24/7 at Horsemanship101.com/Courses

Your Foal: Essential Training

Meet the Author

Keith Hosman, John Lyons Certified Trainer

Keith Hosman lives just outside of San Antonio, Texas and divides his time between writing how-to training materials and conducting training clinics in most of these United States as well as in Germany and the Czech Republic.

Visit his flagship site horsemanship101.com for more D.I.Y. training and to find a clinic happening soon near you.

Made in the USA
Las Vegas, NV
18 October 2021

32595006R00066